OPEN SPACE

Urban Public Landscape Design

OPEN SPACE —— Urban Public Landscape Design
Copyright© Sendpoints Publishing Co., Limited

SendPoints
Publisher: Lin Gengli
Editor in Chief: Lin Shijian
Executive Editor: Cody Chen   Jasmine Tam
Design Director: Lin Shijian
Executive Designer: Lin Qiumei
Proofreading: Sundae Li

Address: Room 15A Block 9 Tsui Chuk Garden, Wong Tai Sin, Kowloon, Hongkong
Tel: +852-35832323
Fax: +852-35832448
Email: info@sendpoint.com.cn
Website: www.sendpoint.com.cn

Distributed by Guangzhou Sendpoints Book Co., Ltd.
Sales Manager: Peng Yanghui(China)   Limbo(International)
Guangzhou   Tel: (86)-02-89095121
Beijing   Tel: (86)-10-84139071
Shanghai   Tel: (86)-21-63523469
Email: export@sendpoint.com.cn
Website: www.sendpoint.com.cn

ISBN 978-988-16834-3-4

Printed and bound in China

How do you define landscape? It can be defined as natural scenery or artificially constructed scenery. Comprised of different ecosystems or transformed/constructed by people, a landscape is a part of the human living environment. Over time, in the East or the West, the emphasis of landscape lies in its visual aesthetics. With the development of economy and technology, land has been used in a variety of ways, among which is landscaping.

Urban public landscape design is within the scope of urban landscape design. Urban landscape is usually an integration of natural and artificial landscape elements, which defines urban public landscape design as the construction or renovation activity by landscape architects. Landscape design requires designers to not only focus on the outline or appearance design of the architecture but also consider integrating the surrounding natural or otherwise elements in the design process. This helps the landscape design to echo with the natural environment while adding functions and aesthetics to the design, and enhancing its overall artistic value.

With the society pacing forward, human beings pay more attention to self-awareness, mental and physical needs. Urban public landscape design should not only consider the harmony with the natural environment, but also needs to pay attention to human physiological and psychological needs, to provide a convenient and pleasant environment, thus to create a harmonious relationship among people, landscape, and nature to achieve a relative balance.

In today's society, unique and pleasant public landscapes are everywhere, among which are renovated parks, squares and beaches with interesting lightings and comfortable loungers. The sustainable development of urban resources becomes the premise of the future development of urban public landscape. Reasonable urban planning and efficient use of public resources manifest the philosophy of the harmony of public landscape design, people, and nature.

This book focuses on urban public landscape design. Combining landscape planning and artistic design, along with related descriptions and high-quality photos and detailed design plan, the editors aim to present the artistic charm of urban public landscapes and the sound relationship among public landscape design, people, and nature in cities.

FOREWORD

In today's global environment all cities face competition on multiple levels regional, national, and in many cases continental and global. To enable a city to work more efficiently, it is tasked with the constant challenge of developing its infrastructure ahead of the economic pace. Even though the concept of sustainability is widely recognised as being pivotal in the creation of new cities and the growth of existing ones the evidence on the ground seems very mixed. The reason for this might be that sustainability is predominantly understood and put into practice as a response to the logic of constructing buildings. This results in sustainability being evaluated only in terms of construction functionality through ecological impacts such as energy efficiency, carbon neutrality and technological innovation -- all measurable by LEED.

The radical question for landscape architects and urban designers in these circumstances needs to be: How can sustainability manifest itself in a green city that is both socially and ecologically sustainable?

As a starting point of thinking about this challenge we could do no better than revisit a period when urbanization was becoming a major force shaping our natural world and creating over a short period of time in premier cities such as New York. This considerable and dramatic rise of American cities happened against the background of the revolutionary turmoil of Europe during the early 19th century, leading to both emigration and the establishment of fairer laws and practices that we take for granted now. England having been at the forefront of the upheavals of industrial revolution, led the way with the abolition of slavery, child labour and in the 1840s the establishment of the first public parks in London and Liverpool. These greatly impressed young American farmer visitor, Fredrick Law Olmstead and became his inspiration for Central Park in NY embodying his social consciousness and commitment to egalitarian ideals. More importantly, Olmstead believed that Central Park as a common green space must be equally accessible to all citizens and consequently he got involved in a long struggle to put into practice a principle that today is fundamental to our concept of a public park. Today, 155 years later, it is difficult to imagine New York functioning without this key public realm.

In addition to working as a landscape architect, Olmstead often assumed the role of a journalist, social critic and public administrator in sharp contrast to the exclusive professionalism of almost all landscape architects working today. As a multifaceted agent of change, Olmstead understood that designs for public projects should not be limited by the financial or physical means of the designer or the commissioner. Believing instead that the proposition of a new park needs to come from a different time frame than that of the immediate present when residents of cities often see public realm projects mostly as a source of needless taxation burden and not believing that they will benefit from a public park in the same capacity as the wealthy. Confronting publicly this belief and creating parks that were meant to be enjoyed by all became the key stone of the thinking of another major figure of its time -- H.W.S. Cleveland. Both he and Olmstead shared a strong commitment to the future believing that a growing population will make open strategic spaces like parks all the more valuable and desirable in all future cities.

Cleveland wrote that, to be successful in the landscape architecture field, one must "Look forward a century, to the time when the city has a population of a million, and think what will be their wants." Sensing the start of a dramatic change in his lifetime, he also wrote a seminal text attempting to describe landscape architecture as central force of the future shaping of our environment. In the preface of Landscape Architecture as Applied to the Wants of the West he wrote:
"The term 'landscape architecture' is objectionable, as being only figuratively expressive of the art it is used to designate. I make use of it, under protest, as the readiest means of making myself understood, in the absence of a more appropriate term. If the art is ever developed to the extent I believe to be within its legitimate limits, it will achieve for itself a name worthy of its position. Until it does so, it is idle to attempt to exalt it in the world's estimation by giving it a high-sounding title."
What would he write today?

I believe he would write about the need for landscape architects to be involved, as a matter of urgency, as proactive mediators in the sustainable green city project. To paraphrase H. W. S. Cleveland today we need to "Look forward a century, to the time when the world has a population 9 billion by 2100, and think what will be their wants."

Today all cities involve one crucial and common resource -- their people. The global magnetism of a premier city stems not only from its infrastructure, but also from the power and energy it draws from those who live and work in it, and so sustain it. Consequently, the notion of social and cultural sustainability defined as "Liveability" needs to be seen as one of the core qualities of any city and as a primary catalyst for its sustainable future. The search for inclusive social and cultural sustainability on the scale of cities will require its more holistic examination, as a more collaboratively based search. A new look at an enlightened self-preservation from within should pervade our thinking and this I believe will require a radical rethink of the manner in which our cities are shaped today predominantly by architects and planners designing in a predominantly Western technology based tradition with little or no regard to the embodied geography and cultural / social identity of specific locations.

At a time when China, India, Brazil are undergoing dramatic and accelerated urbanization, landscape architecture needs to bring to forefront its understanding of time in terms of nature and eco systems and link this knowledge to a sense of place and community. The application of this psycho geographical understanding by landscape architects within a broadly based multi disciplinary collaborative approach to urbanism is, I believe, a key to unlocking the impact of a green city that is both socially and ecologically sustainable.

The understanding of the different meanings of the fast solid (architecture) and the slower and more complex (void) the landscape in sustainable green city is the key to unlocking its impact on the planet with its fast diminishing resources of energy, productive land and water.
As proactive mediators, landscape architects need to blur the boundaries between culture, design and ecology to embody a wide range of interests in the creation of the public realm.
Whether it is the creation of a public square, a street, park or infrastructure, we need to recognise that one person cannot achieve this alone. Landscape architects need to start forming more integrated working relationship with real communities as well as opening opportunities for the input of others be it economists, social scientists, agronomists, and artists, etc.
The resulting multifaceted and culturally informed response might become the start of a more holistic grounding of the sustainable green cities of the present and future. In this context it is clear that the task of developing socially vibrant communities is a vital aspect of sustainable urbanism as only through the development of inclusive communities will people as citizens start committing to the sustainability agenda itself. The design and meaning of inspiring public spaces in our cities need to transform our cities, making them green both literally in an environmental sense, and metaphorically as places of new growths and positive changes. This will require challenging the way sustainability is being delivered and understood today, opening up a space where truly sustainable developments are such that will grow, adapt and transform cities for decades to come.

Peter Fink
Director
FoRM Associates

Contemporary urban form typically experienced in unique locations is unified through connectivity, integration of sustainable approaches, incorporation of cultural contexts, art and employment of the exaggerated naturalized element as a tool within existing dense urban fabrics to create critical sequences integral to the development of contemporary open spaces and paths. The following five projects consider concepts of open space in a range of physical and perceptual realms, incorporating issues of technology, artifice and sustainability as they impact their specific urban context.

The delicate and the monumental, the natural and the artificial, the sublime and the obvious are considered in relation to public space — the realm of the average person, where individuals, families, units, communities exchange ideas and communicate shared values.

California Academy of Sciences, San Francisco, United States
The California Academy of Sciences incorporates science as performance space including live habitats, recycling, information exchange and the regeneration of energy communicating directly with the viewer as the building's concept to develop its overall architectural form. The architecture includes a field of wild flowers, natural irrigation systems and photovoltaics among other significant sustainable approaches. Its formal approach is emblematic of the local topography and unique ecosystems in a two and half acre green roof. As an educational system, cohesive open and closed spaces are used as tools for representation and an occupiable architectural diagram is constructed by Renzo Piano.

River Manzanares Lineal Park, Madrid, Spain
A project to organize five miles of the banks of the River Manzanares through the concept of connectivity and counterpoints to the human scale, passes through the city becoming a virtual idealized urban utopian city, where all that is good exists. Involving 284 acres of parks, a dozen bridges and 14.8 acres of public and sports facilities, interpretation environments, art centers, and an urban beach, children's areas and cafes, the restoration of the hydraulic architectural heritage and naturalized and artificial elements, issues of monumentality and representation elevate the role of public space and the experience of the river in this project.

The river, a literal metaphor and tool to reconnect and suture the city, is considered in successive scales and approaches, territories and strategies, local and specific. The project establishes a physical and conceptual continuity at three primary points. It is a linear superstructure; the first Unit of Landscape: the Salón de Pinos includes a green corridor which organizes the continuity of the paths. The Monumental Scene, the second Unit of Landscape, creates a connection through negative space with the concept of the Panoramic Scene, a visceral implied grand scale shift that reflects upon the elevated space of the Palacio Real and the origin of the city. The third Unit of Landscape is the largest park in the project and incorporates formal and narrative elements through various constructs of water, utilizing the river in its purest form through fountains, and a path between the Matadero and the park as a continuous element connecting the river to the city.

Seafront of Benidorm, Spain

The Seafront of Benidorm, a public open space, creates an environment dependent on play and artifice between the natural and the urban at a natural threshold, the seafront at Benidorm. This deliberate use of physical elements of lines and movement creates artificial constructs that unify the space between the ocean and the land providing opportunities in plan and in section to be explored by the public. A sinuous colorful promenade links town and sea, above and below, areas for contemplation and recreation, resonating with the phenomenal qualities of the ocean and the scale of the town. This project depends on the unified experience of the gesture to express a cohesive idea of this place, one that draws from the uniqueness of Benidorm.

Benidorm is a city of an extremely high density concentrated in a tiny territory, where the promenade is one and a half kilometers. The organic expression of the elements provides a literal reference to the ocean waves, while the color added to the surface recalls a two-dimensional drawing technique and expression of its own. Various levels and platforms provide areas for play, meeting, leisure and programming. A sustainable approach to the development of the levels from structural, to natural incorporates support for separation of naturalized edges and programming for longevity of the project.

The public engagement with the project is likely to draw in more users over time as the depth of thought and experience is further understood.

Whatami, Rome, Italy

Artifice and play, performance space and "green" are formalized into a cultural landscape in a museum setting, Whatami. Colorful animated artificial flowers attract the public to this urban landscape.

The museum utilizes performance and exhibition in the program development, recognizing the inherent nature of the city and creates a place for these activities to occur within its environment. Utilizing the construct of a hill, an artificial landscape is created for performance and event. The archipelago-hill, generate smaller green areas in the garden and potentially outside the museum, working as a garden, injecting "green" into the concrete plateau of the museum's outdoor space, allows it to serve as a stage for concerts and other events, or as a space to rest and look at the museum itself, a reflective space, a place to consider entering the museum.

Large "flowers" provide shadow during the day and light at night, resulting in a public cityscape that is occupied 24 hours a day. The project integrates into the city through multiple approaches, where surprise points of view illuminate opportunities previously unknown to the patron.

Young Circle ArtsPark, Hollywood, Florida, United States

A perfect circle is deconstructed in downtown Hollywood, Florida, where history, architecture, a park, urban space, a constructed landscape and experience evolve and are linked through a unique art and topographic exchange in an urban environment. A woven historic pathway organically traces a route through African Baobabs, Florida Live Oaks and orange blooming Poinciana's, linking Florida's cultural history to a global community and the urban spaces' new contemporary architecture and program. Cantilevered concrete Visual Arts Pavilion emerges from the earth connecting the ground and sky to a Performing Arts Pavilion and ten acres of adjusted ground planes and altered landscapes. Inspired by local bromeliads, terraced gardens provide spontaneous performances under the sound sculpture by Ritsuko Taho, Millennium Springs, through replayed sounds of electromagnetic sound waves of the Baobab tree.

The ArtsPark at Young Circle, Hollywood includes public architecture and spaces that inspire play and cultural activities, provide respite amidst sound and water elements, include formal landscaped gardens, shaded respite under mature trees or animated play in the Children's playground in a verdant Florida setting. The Performing Arts Pavilion provides events on lawn or chair seating available for over two thousand people or amphitheater visual arts programming, from glass blowing to metal studio workshops and exhibitions can be inspired by the environment and is available to the public.

Public space is open space — a vital ground for recreation, reconnection and respite. Through art, landscape and architecture, open spaces provide the city with a satellite territory where individuals become part of the public consciousness. Each is elevated and reconnected.

Open space yet connected, public, yet individual, peaceful, yet social. Spaces for people and spaces for all, spaces for cities allow for a seamless transition between the city and itself. In this new realm we become more conscious of our human nature, our senses and perceptions awaken, our surroundings become stage like and our activities become idolized while connections are highlighted as we share a common ground with each other.

Margi Nothard
Design Principal + President
Glavovic Studio Inc.

CONTENTS

INDEX

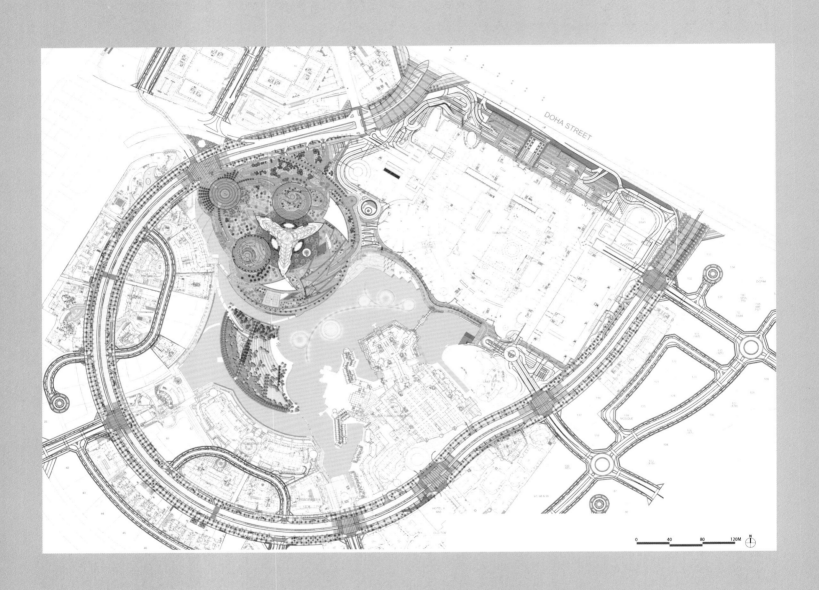

DOHA STREET

0   40   80   120M   N

Design Agency: SWA Group
Designer: John L. Wong, Hui-Li Lee
Photography: David Gal, Tom Fox
Location: Dubai, UAE
Area: 110, 000 m²

Burj Khalifa Tower Park

General Description:

Situated on 11 hectares of land, the "green oasis" encircling the Burj Khalifa tower includes plazas, gardens, pools and promenades that create a human-scale frame for the tallest tower in the world.

Design Concept:

Given that humans have been inhabiting some of the most unlivable places on Earth for thousands of years, this project set out to pay tribute to human life in the desert by creating a stunning green space that works with the desert climate instead of against it, resulting in a world-class space that is accessible and enjoyable for humans but still mindful of the remarkable beauty and history of this unique environment.

Design Details:

Creating a landscape around a complicated, iconic, and large building required a thorough understanding of the building's multiple functions and inherent mixed-use nature, as well as the multi-model traffic coordination that adjacency to a bustling urban center entailed. Multiple entries and drop-offs, service access points, garage and structural considerations, and public versus private entrances were just some of the many circulation nodes that needed to be considered on the ground level, prompting the design of clear navigation and wayfinding graphics to direct visitors towards building entrances as well as public oasis, cooling, and garden areas. Each circulatory system had to be carefully designed and sequenced for the project to function seamlessly, but also had to be cognizant of the nuanced social interactions in Islamic culture.

Beyond the choreography of various circulation and access paths,

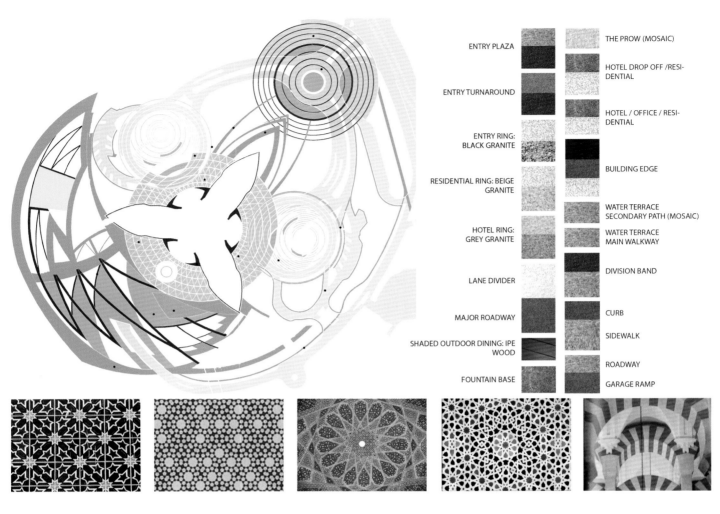

ENTRY PLAZA

ENTRY TURNAROUND

ENTRY RING:
BLACK GRANITE

RESIDENTIAL RING: BEIGE
GRANITE

HOTEL RING:
GREY GRANITE

LANE DIVIDER

MAJOR ROADWAY

SHADED OUTDOOR DINING: IPE
WOOD

FOUNTAIN BASE

THE PROW (MOSAIC)

HOTEL DROP OFF /RESI-
DENTIAL

HOTEL / OFFICE / RESI-
DENTIAL

BUILDING EDGE

WATER TERRACE
SECONDARY PATH (MOSAIC)

WATER TERRACE
MAIN WALKWAY

DIVISION BAND

CURB

SIDEWALK

ROADWAY

GARAGE RAMP

LEGEND

MAIN ENTRY / WATER COURT ARRIVAL
1. PALM TREE GROVE AT ENTRY PLAZA
2. WATER PETALS
3. SCULPTURAL FOUNTAIN
4. SPECIAL STONE PAVING
5. SEASONAL COLORS
6. ENTRY SIGNAGE

TOWER GARDEN ZONE
7. INFORMAL CANOPY FLOWERING SHADE TREES
8. FLOWERING SHRUBS & GROUNDCOVER
9. STONE TERRACE WALLS
10. PALM LINED MEDIAN / ROAD

HOTEL ENTRY ARRIVAL COURT
11. STEEL ENCLOSURE WALL WITH NIGHT LUMINATION
12. ENTRY FOUNTAIN
13. CENTRAL PALM GROVE
14. SEASONAL COLORS IN RADIAL PATTERN
15. COBBLE STONE DRIVEWAY
16. SPECIAL STONE PAVING AND INTRICATE BANDING
17. SPECIAL MOSAIC PAVING RING

RESIDENTIAL ENTRY ARRIVAL COURT
18. WOODEN ENCLOSURE WALL WITH NIGHT LUMINATION
19. ENTRY FOUNTAIN
20. SPECIAL FLOWERING TREE GROVE
21. SEASONAL COLORS WITH PALM CIRCLE
22. SPECIAL STONE PAVING
23. COBBLE STONE DRIVEWAY
24. SPECIAL MOSAIC PAVING RING
25. VISITOR PARKING
26. GARDEN

LAKE FRONT RECREATION
27. GRAND VIEWING DECK WITH SPECIAL GARDEN PARTERRE.
28. WATER FEATURE/PALM GROVE @ LOWER ARRIVAL COURT
29. SPECIAL INDIGENOUS FLOWERING SHADE TREES
30. INFORMAL SEATING
31. SHADE CANOPY STRUCTURE
32. PLANES OF REFLECTING WATER POOL CASCADING WITH
    GRAVITY FLOW
33. SLOPPED GARDEN WALKS WITH FLOWERING BORDERS
34. OUTDOOR EATING ISLAND INCORPORATING MAJOR CANOPY
35. LANDSCAPE FLOWERING / LAWN PARTERRES INTERSECT
    WITH WATER
36. FLOWER GARDENS
37. PLANTING WALL AT GARAGE ENTRY
38. VIEWING LAWN TERRACE
39. KID'S WATER PLAY
40. SEATING WALL & STAIRS
41. AMPHITHEATER
42. BOCCE COURT
43. TENNIS COURTS WITH VINE PLANTING ENCLOSURE
44. PALM LINED WALKWAY
45. WATERFRONT SEATING & STEPS

0   25   50   75M

there were coordination complexities induced by fixed design elements such as emergency exits, intake and exhaust vents, and structural beams and girders, as well as the sequencing challenge of designing the surface landscape while subterranean parking structures were in the midst of construction.

The inspiration for the Burj Khalifa groundscape was the intricate and beautiful patterning found in the region's Islamic art, architecture, and gardens. Indigenous plant materials and local stone paving are woven across the groundplane in a complex geometric pattern reminiscent of the region's spider lilies as well as the formal gardens and mosques that spread throughout the gulf region. By using native plantings and sustainable water features for cooling and comfort, the project aims to improve the micro-climates surrounding the building and provide respite from an exceedingly hot desert climate. Water in the Emirates is scarce and becoming scarcer; in addition to using low water/drought tolerant native plant species, the design of a state-of-the-art irrigation system that uses recycled water from the tower's cooling equipment helped to ensure efficient usage of this precious resource while still reducing the heat island effects on the ground, cooling the air with extensive softscape, and providing shade and mitigating glare with an extensive tree canopy comprised of more than 15 different species, including Date Palms, Silver Buttonwood, Banyan Trees, Olive Trees, and Laurels. Besides the environmental benefits, the use of indigenous plantings and locally-sourced materials arrayed in patterns that reference Islamic aesthetics further the theme of locality by providing a culturally and historically aligned counterpoint to the stark modernism of the tower itself.

The project required in-depth design and technical expertise in the areas of hydrological engineering, horticulture, international building codes and construction standards, and materials sourcing. In addition, members of the design team spent several multi-day research trips in Dubai researching plant materials by visiting local and regional nurseries as well as nearby projects to develop a plant palette that works in this extreme climate.

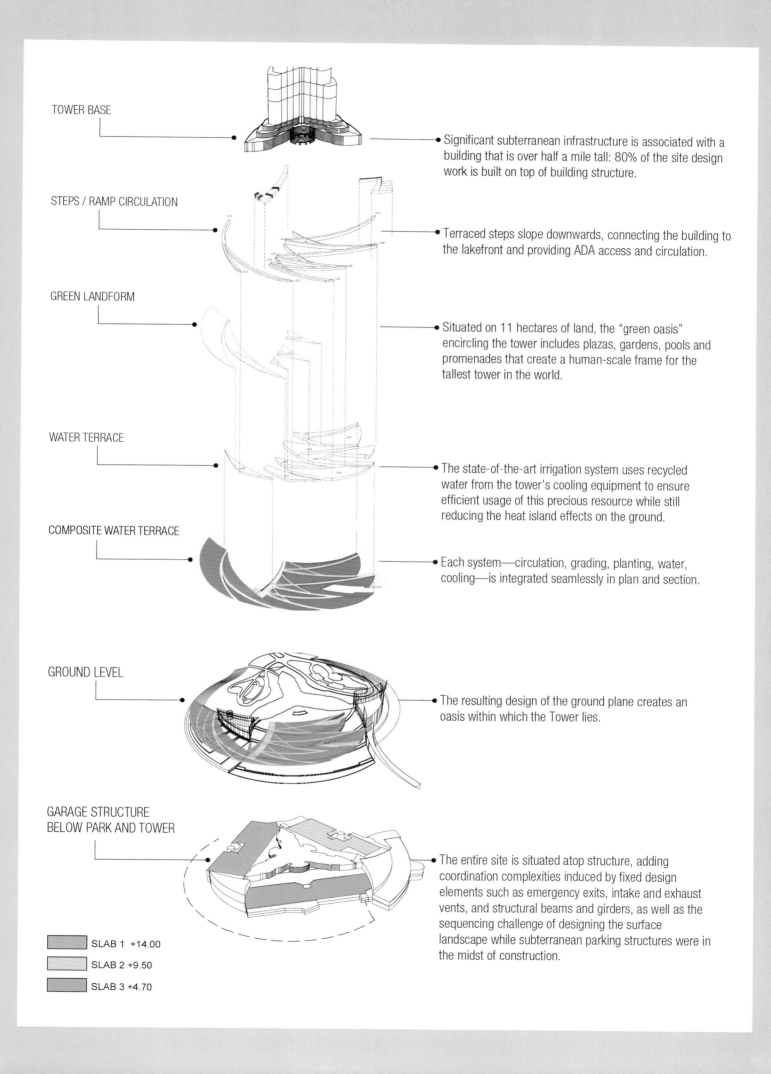

TOWER BASE

Significant subterranean infrastructure is associated with a building that is over half a mile tall: 80% of the site design work is built on top of building structure.

STEPS / RAMP CIRCULATION

Terraced steps slope downwards, connecting the building to the lakefront and providing ADA access and circulation.

GREEN LANDFORM

Situated on 11 hectares of land, the "green oasis" encircling the tower includes plazas, gardens, pools and promenades that create a human-scale frame for the tallest tower in the world.

WATER TERRACE

The state-of-the-art irrigation system uses recycled water from the tower's cooling equipment to ensure efficient usage of this precious resource while still reducing the heat island effects on the ground.

COMPOSITE WATER TERRACE

Each system—circulation, grading, planting, water, cooling—is integrated seamlessly in plan and section.

GROUND LEVEL

The resulting design of the ground plane creates an oasis within which the Tower lies.

GARAGE STRUCTURE
BELOW PARK AND TOWER

The entire site is situated atop structure, adding coordination complexities induced by fixed design elements such as emergency exits, intake and exhaust vents, and structural beams and girders, as well as the sequencing challenge of designing the surface landscape while subterranean parking structures were in the midst of construction.

SLAB 1 +14.00

SLAB 2 +9.50

SLAB 3 +4.70

The inspiration for the Burj Khalifa groundscape was the intricate and beautiful patterning found in the region's Islamic art, architecture, and gardens. By using native plantings and sustainable water features for cooling and comfort, the project aims to improve the micro-climate surrounding the building and provide respite from an exceedingly hot desert climate.

CALIFORNIA ACADEMY OF SCIENCES
SITE PLAN
1"=30'

Design Agency: SWA Group
Designer: Renzo Piano Building Workshop
Photography: Tom Fox, SWA Group
Location: San Francisco, USA
Area: 38, 445 m²

California Academy of Sciences

General Description:

One of San Francisco's first sustainable building projects, the new California Academy of Sciences supports a stunning 2.5-acre green roof. Emphasizing habitat quality and connectivity, the project has received LEED Platinum certification.

Design Concept:

This project focuses on sustainable design. The Academy's commitment to sustainability and their location

in San Francisco's mild climate provide an ideal opportunity to incorporate sustainable design strategies into the construction plan. Sustainable design was followed not only in the energy efficient heating and cooling of the building, but also in the choice of materials, location of spaces, re-use and efficient use of water and even the generation of energy as integral to the building design and construction. Sustainability will also be part of the exhibitions,

the organizational philosophy, and the day-to-day operations. The public will be able to see and understand many of the principles of sustainable design.

Design Details:

About the green roof construction, over the roof's waterproofing and building insulation, a grid of intercept drains was created using narrow, rock-filled baskets (gabion) set and connected end-to-end. In the sloped conditions, the gabion grid provides support for the pre-planted, biodegradable trays laid by hand. The 75 mm deep, coconut husk (coir), planting trays containing four native perennial and five native annuals, were pre-grown offsite. When the established plant trays were ready for shipping they were carefully stacked in bakery racks, and trucked to the site. The racks were then craned to the roof and the pre-planted

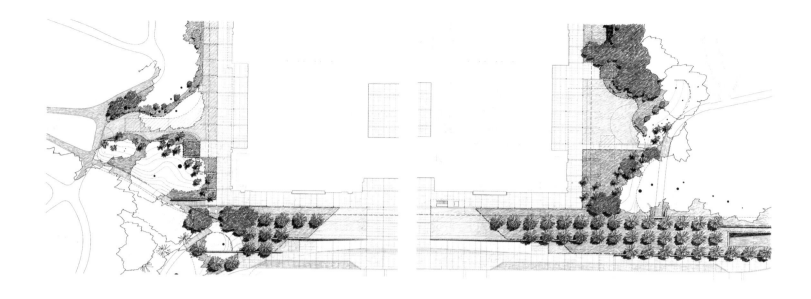

trays set on an additional 75 mm layer of planting media, over reservoir/drainage board within the gabion grid. The biodegradable coir trays provided temporary support structure until the plants became established on the rooftop, and as the coir trays breakdown, they become part of the planting media.

About the sustainability design, a model of technical and natural systems working harmoniously, the roof features numerous sustainable design elements. The California native plants that carpet the building were chosen for their adaptability to the Bay Area's seasonal irrigation cycle. The plants were also selected to attract local butterflies, birds and insects, some of them endangered. The roof is designed to thrive on natural, not mechanical irrigation sources. In addition to this water-conscious approach to planting, the water that does collect and run off the roof will be recycled back into the water table. The roof provides sustainable energy resources too. Photovoltaic cells line the roof perimeter, collecting solar energy to help power the Academy. The main sustainable features include energy efficiency, daylight, water efficiency, indoor air quality, etc.

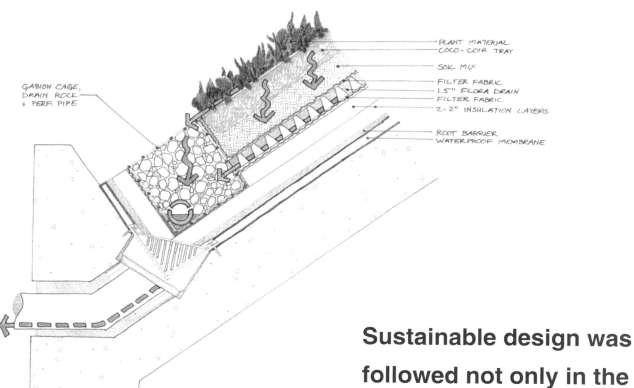

GABION CAGE,
DRAIN ROCK
+ PERF. PIPE

PLANT MATERIAL
COCO-COIR TRAY
SOIL MIX
FILTER FABRIC
1.5" FLORA DRAIN
FILTER FABRIC
2-2" INSULATION LAYERS

ROOT BARRIER
WATERPROOF MEMBRANE

Sustainable design was followed not only in the energy efficient heating and cooling of the building, but also in the choice of materials, location of spaces, re-use and efficient use of water and even the generation of energy as integral to the building design and construction.

Design Agency: FoRM Associates
Photography: Chris McAleese, FoRM Associates
Location: London, UK
Area: 270,000 m²

Northala Fields Park

General Description:

Northala Fields is the largest new London park for a century. Arguably the most significant feature of the Northala Fields design is the construction of a new monumental landform on site, utilizing substantial volumes of imported construction rubble from a pool of London-wide development projects such as Heathrow Terminal 5, White City and Wembley Stadium.

Design Concept:

The approach to the design of Northala Fields has been a careful balance of providing a significant contribution to biodiversity in the area, while ensuring that the design meets the requirements to minimize potential bird strike hazard to aircraft from the nearby Northolt Aerodrome.

Design Details:

The park incorporates fully accessible fishing ponds, two children's playgrounds, a marshland reserve, a model boating pond, cycle paths, open playing fields, and the four giant mounds.

The new landform provides a solution to a number of site and development issues; mitigation of impact from the adjoining A40 (particularly noise, visual and air pollution); the provision of new

36

recreation opportunities not currently available in the generally flat London Park; and the creation of new ecological opportunities through new topography and soils.

Four large conical earth mounds along the A40 edge of the site help to reduce visual and noise pollution and provide a major piece of "land art" that is a landmark gateway for West London. In particular, the viewpoint on top of the tallest mound provides a 360-degree panoramic view of the surrounding area including central London and Canary Wharf.

A series of clearly defined key routes support recreational uses and activities of the new neighborhood park. A network of primary and secondary paths connects with adjacent open spaces that make up the rest of the Countryside Park. New playground is set along the central spine of the park along with a series of open meadows and semi-formal planting and seating areas for more contemplative activities. Water is another major feature of the park, with a network of six interconnecting fishing lakes, a model boating lake and wildlife ponds, streams and wetlands.

Enhancing the ecological values of the site has also been a focus of the new design. A range of new habitats was created: Woodland both around the perimeter and within the site adds to the diversity of the existing woodland habitat; meadow and grassland types are the dominant vegetation in the development; water and wetland in the form of new watercourses provide opportunities for water and wetland flora and fauna that are not presented on the site. Each mound has been created with varying soil conditions that support wild flowers and grass seeds to give four distinct habitats.

One of the values of the project is that it increased the biodiversity of the area by using different earths in the four large conical earth mounds to provide habitants for different species.

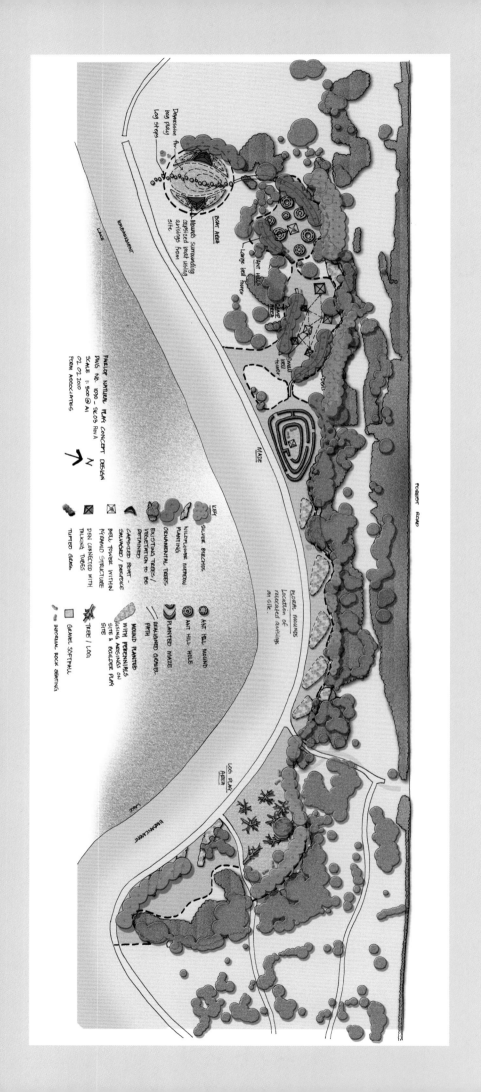

Design Agency: FoRM Associates

Photography: FoRM Associates

Location: London, UK

Area: 40,000 m²

Fairlop Waters Park

General Description:

This natural play area is located in the northern area of Fairlop Waters Country Park. The design provides a natural and adventurous play experience for children in particular 8 – 13 years age group.

Design Concept:

The design focuses on selected areas with maximum potential for imaginative play integrating with existing trees and vegetation as a natural setting. The resulting narrative emphasizes an interlinked series of hidden spaces to encourage exploration and discovery.

Design Details:

The natural play area draws on the geology and soil conditions of the space, alluding to the history of the space as a boating lake and Fairlop Fair, and connecting it to the adjacent Boulder Play area and lake. The zones are a sequence of activities and functions aimed to tapping into both the physical and creative aspects of children's play by creating spaces which challenge them physically — for example through climbing, balancing, running, jumping — as well as such functions as experimental, experiential and educational spaces which stimulate their imagination, and encourage them to make up their own stories and scenarios. The aim was to create stimulating environments which invite children to take a hands-on approach to explore their

surroundings as well as inclusive social interaction. The design provides an environment where parents and carers can monitor the children's activities without affecting the atmosphere of natural play.

The zones are linked together through consistency of materials, such as timber species for all timber structures, bespoke bell towers each with a different tone when struck for interactive play between play zones, woodland planting in the overall site backdrop and swards of wildflower meadow planting throughout. The site also borrows from the material palette of adjacent Boulder Play site, namely Coxwell gravel for the soft-fall area to the Log Play and smaller boulders for informal seating.

The aim was to create
stimulating environments
which invite children to take a
hands-on approach to explore
their surroundings as well as
inclusive social interaction.

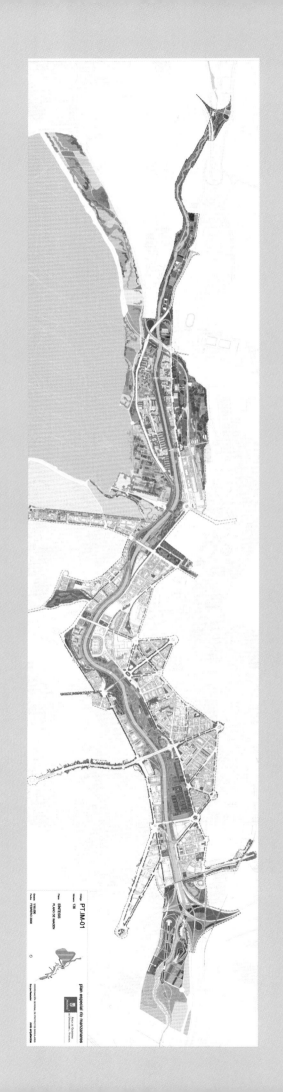

PT.IM-01

Código:
Número: 138

Plano: SINTESIS
PLANO DE IMAGEN

Escala: 1:50.000
Fecha: FEBRERO 2008

plan especial río manzanares

Architects: *Burgos & Garrido Arquitectos, Porras & La Casta, Rubio & Álvarez-Sala, West 8*

Team Director: *Ginés Garrido*

Photography: *Ana Müller, Jeroen Musch, Municipality of Madrid*

Location: *Madrid, Spain*

Area: *1, 200, 000 m²*

46-55

River Manzanares Lineal Park

General Description:

The project, also called the Madrid Río (Madrid River), includes organizing the 5 miles of the banks of the River Manzanares that passes through the city, the design of 115 ha of parks, a dozen bridges and 6 ha of public and sports facilities, interpretation and art centers, an urban beach, children's areas and cafés, and the restoration of the hydraulic architectural heritage. In addition, a master plan was drafted for an area of 880 ha which will give a prominent role to the public space in the districts closest to the river.

Design Concept:

The strategy of the project was based on the conviction that through the river it would be possible to connect the city, the greatest expression of artificial action, with the land to the north and south of Madrid, in which the natural elements inherent to the river basin still survive. It was conceived in successive approaches or scales, on which the considerations of the field of play were applied, obtaining varied answers and solutions, from the territorial or strategic, to the local or specific.

Design Details:

The project establishes a physical and conceptual continuity, which did not previously exist, between the city center and the valuable countryside that surrounds it, and as a result the River Manzanares has been transformed into the point that connects the city with its geography. It also has been highly complex and the solution is fulfilled in the three main units of landscape.

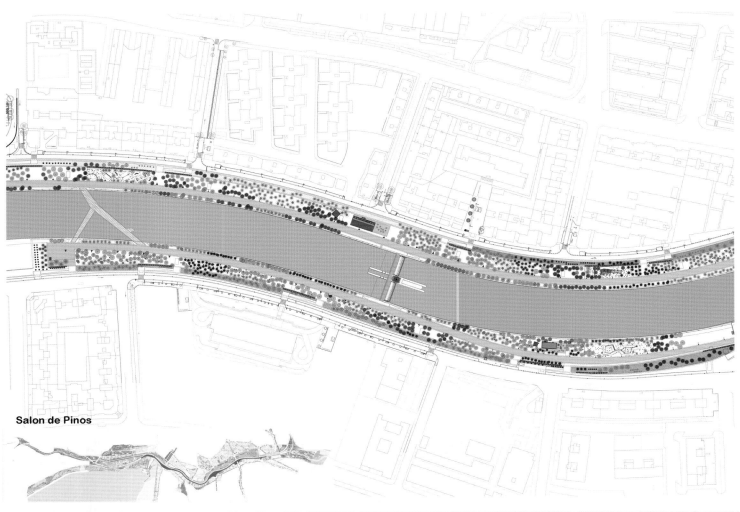

Salon de Pinos

First unit of landscape: the Salón de Pinos

The Salón de Pinos, or green corridor, passes by the right bank of the river and its linear superstructure is the element that organizes the continuity of the paths along the right bank of the river. It is almost entirely built above the tunnels and has an average width of 30 meters. Over the concrete slab covering the roadway, more than 9,000 units of different species of pine have been planted, of diverse sizes, shapes and groupings within a framework of woodland planting. The activities incorporated into the Salón are done so with a coherent language akin to the forest. A clear example of this procedure is the set of children's play areas, which are specifically designed as a complete system of natural forms.

Second unit of landscape: the monumental scene

It is the definitive connection of the old town with the Casa de Campo, a woodland park of more than 1,700 hectares. The new form of contact, which is now possible thanks to the cars disappearing underground, has been solved through various interventions that take on the monumental and panoramic nature of the area, where the elevated

cross section slow path

cross section fast path

cross section dry river

skirting of the Palacio Real (the first seed of the founding of the city) makes contact with the river.

Third unit of landscape: the riverbed (Arganzuela and Matadero)

On the left bank the course of the river separates itself from the city. The main project on this bank is the new Parque de la Arganzuela, built over the former communal pasture meadows. In these surroundings the Matadero Municipal (Municipal Slaughterhouse) was built, as a notable example of post-industrial architecture of the second decade of the twentieth century. With the underground tunneling of the motorway, Madrid now had at this point 33 hectares of free space at its disposal, making up the largest park of the project. In the park, a football pitch has been included, as well as two skating rinks and three large children's play areas. Following the left bank of the river, a humid green strip is set out, with a meadow sloping down towards the river. A group of ornamental

Plan detail

Section

Plan

Avenida de Portugal

fountains and a set of three elliptical sheets of pure water introduce this element as a narrative material relating the different associations of vegetation. Each fountain presents a different sonorousness and visual game and is surrounded by little slopes planted with fruit trees that refer to the image of the gardens of legends or of paradise. Across the paths one can access the buildings of the old slaughterhouse, whose refurbishment was completed in April 2011. The design of the paths allows an understanding of the relationship between the Matadero and the park as a continuous element between the river and the city.

In addition, the implementation of bridges over the Manzanares was undertaken as a strategy concerning the whole project, that is to say, as a set in which each element solves specific problems detected in the nearby surroundings, but also in turn, forms part of an integral system of transversal connectivity in accordance with the relationship between the city and the river.

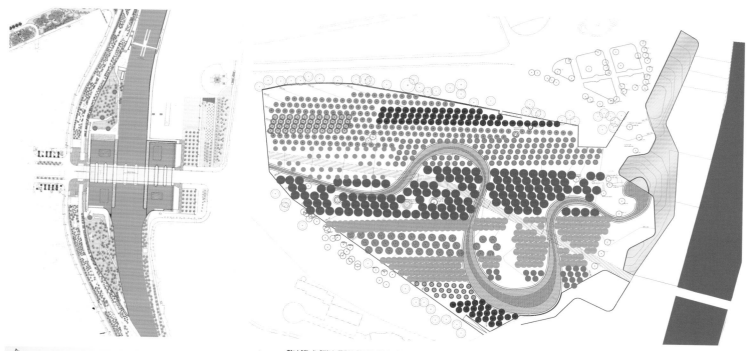

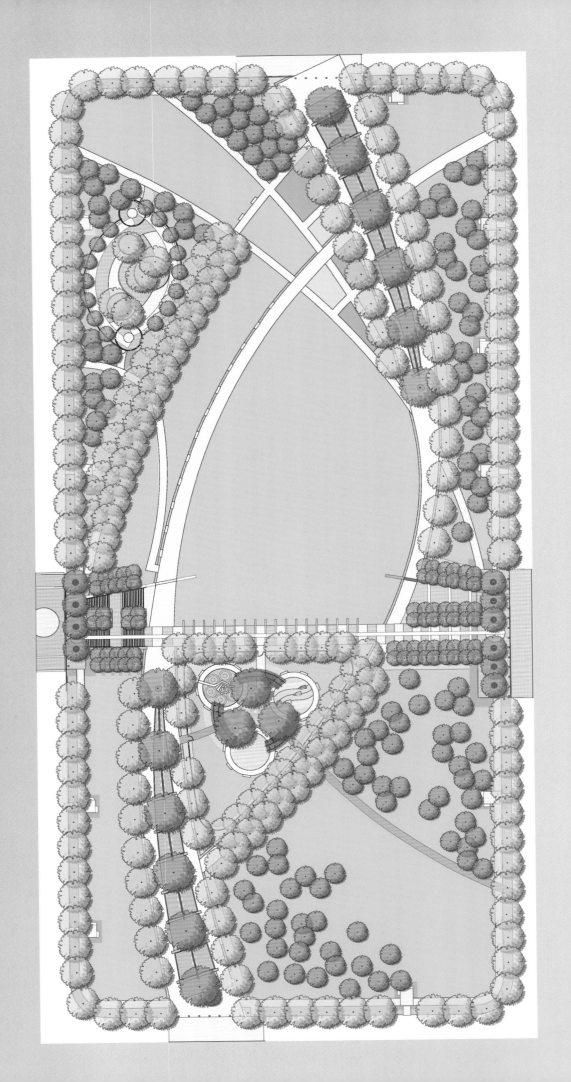

Design Agency: The Office of James Burnett

Designer: James D. Burnett

Photography: James Steinkamp, David B. Seide, The

Office of James Burnett

Location: Chicago, USA

Area: 21, 448 m²

The Park at Lakeshore East

General Description:

The Park at Lakeshore East is the central amenity of a 28-acre community near downtown Chicago at the confluence of Lake Michigan and the Chicago River. The Park at Lakeshore East demonstrates the significant impact of a landscape architectural project that spurs development. It will become an integral part of Chicago's open space network.

Design Concept:

This Park has played an integral part in the continued success of the community and demonstrates the ability of carefully designed open space to enhance growth and create a successful community feature.

Design Details:

The most significant challenge to the creation of successful pedestrian environments the three-tiered street system that surrounds the development, which separates through traffic on lower levels and local traffic on upper levels.

The three-tiered transit system results in a daunting grade change of approximately 25 ft. from the south side of the site to the north. To mitigate this condition, OJB created a grand overlook that offers a commanding view of the park and reinforces the axial connection to Grant Park. A minimalist arrangement of pavers carries the axis of North Field Street down the generous limestone staircase, through the park and into an intimate plaza at the north end of the site. A study in form and geometry, the plaza continues the form language of the axial connection and extrudes it into the third dimension through the addition of seat walls set in plinths of decomposed granite and surrounded by mixed understory plantings. "Cleveland Select" Pears reinforce the axis and strengthen the formal organization of the plaza.

Inspired by the curves of the sailboats that dot Lake Michigan, two sweeping promenades serve as the primary east-west circulation across the site. Each promenade features a series of five fountain basins. Stainless steel weirs pierce the red granite walls and spill water over the rough-hewn Lannon stone basin into stainless grates below, allowing passers-by to cool themselves on a warm summer day. Large basalt stones line the bottom of

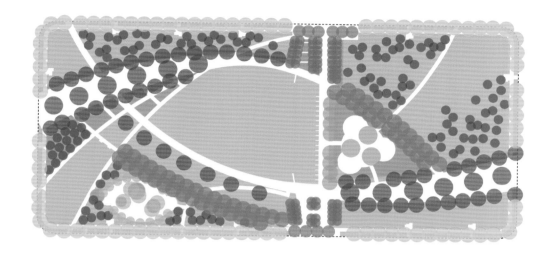

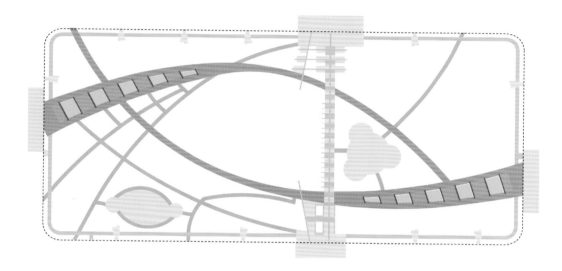

the basins, providing sculptural interest during the fierce Chicago winter while the fountains will lay dormant. Various ornamental plants celebrate the horticultural history of Chicago and provide changing seasonal displays of color. A series of botanical courts extend along the western water garden echoes the form and proportion of the promenades.

Occupying the interstitial space created by the intersection of the promenades and the North Grant axis, the children's garden is organized by a circular plaza with an interactive water feature and safety play surfacing. Three smaller plazas with individual play themes are arranged around the perimeter of the plaza, allowing children to play and wander throughout the spaces. Small, intimate perennial gardens offer a tactile, child-scale garden experience while the surrounding lawn areas provide overflow space for additional activities.

Located along the transitional slope near the south side of the park, the dog park offers a safe, secure area for owners to play with their dogs. Thornless Honey Locusts emerge from three sod-covered berms that emphasize the six-foot grade change across the dog park. Slicing through the highest of the berms, a low stone fountain wall spills water into a meandering runnel that collects at base of the smallest mound. Dogs jockey for position at the drinking bowl and chase each other across the simple, geometric pattern of gravel, unit pavers and colored concrete at all hours of the day and night.

Inspired by the curves of the sailboats that dot Lake Michigan, two sweeping promenades serve as the primary east-west circulation across the site.

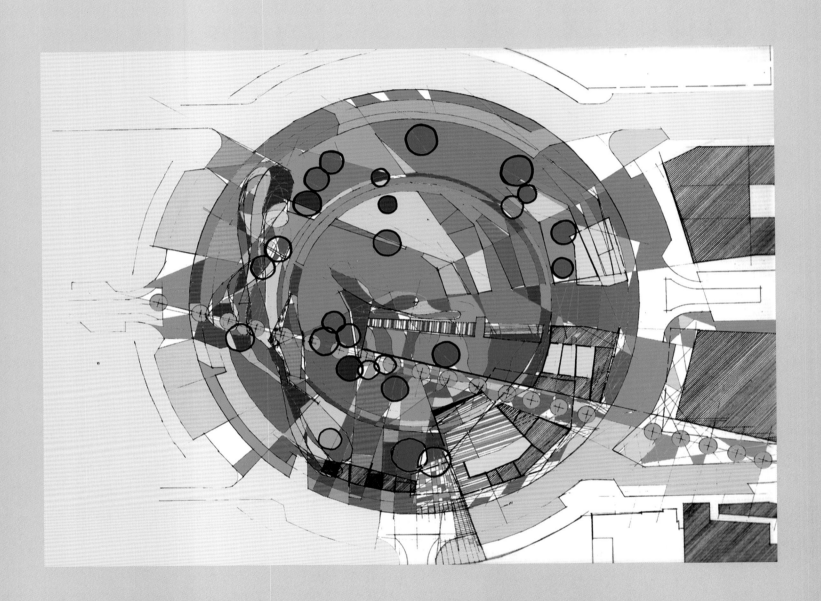

Design Agency: Glavovic Studio Inc.

Designer: Margi Nothard

Photography: Robin Hill

Location: Florida, USA

Area: 40, 469 m²

Young Circle ArtsPark

General Description:

The ArtsPark at Young Circle is a significant urban design and cultural project located in South Florida, in downtown Hollywood. It is a 10-acre innovative cultural arts destination and passive landscaped environment.

Design Concept:

The park concept embraces the vision to link the natural environment of the existing trees and the creative spirit of art in an articulated landscape, through the integration of unique and interactive elements, for everyone in the community to connect to. It is also important to celebrate the distinctive aspects of this environment, especially the unique Baobab trees, while exploring the layering of senses and creating many opportunities for users to spend time in the park to connect to each other and the architecture of the history of Hollywood's Lakes District.

Design Details:

The ArtsPark Buildings include two pavilions, the Visual Arts Pavilion, providing the public options for community classes, a glass blowing studio, metal studio, painting studio, exhibit and classroom and support facilities, outdoor covered classroom spaces and the Performing Arts Pavilion with lawn seating, state of the Art stage, equipment and support spaces.

The park immerses its visitors in a sensory environment through architecture, landscape, with Visual and Performing Arts and Community engaging activities.

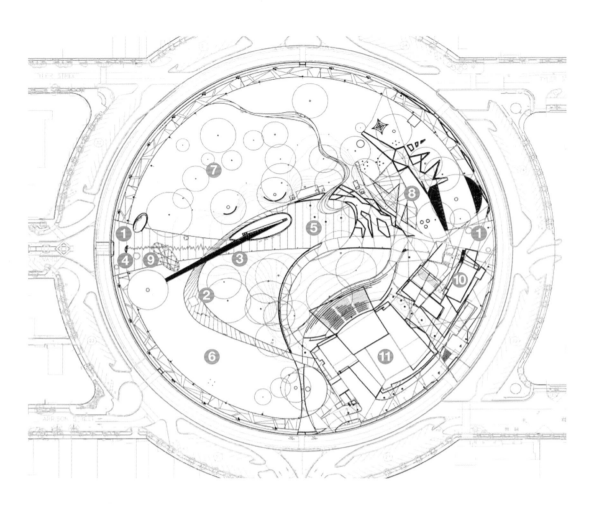

1. East + West Entrance
2. Historic Pavilion
3. Millenium Springs Sculpture
4. Joseph Young Bust
5. Grand Plaza
6. Meadow
7. Grove
8. Children's Area
9. Palm Court
10. Visual Arts Pavilion
    [under construction]
11. Performing Art Building
    [phase 03]
    [ground breaking TBD]

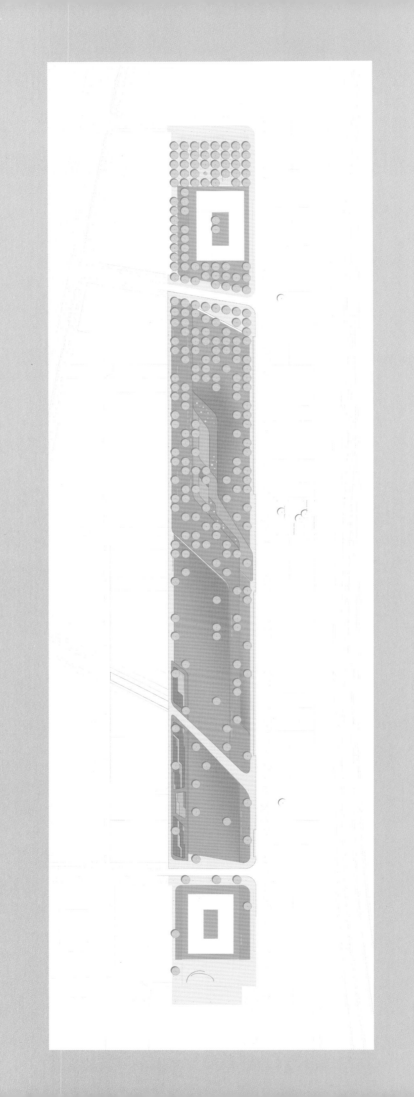

Design Agency: realgrün Landschaftsarchitekten

Designer: Wolf D. Auch, Klaus-D. Neumann

Photography: realgrün Landschaftsarchitekten

Location: Munich, Germany

Area: 39,000 m²

Arnulfpark

General Description:

The project area is part of a former railroad property near Munich central station. On this site a new accommodation was developed.

Design Concept:

The main motion lines react to surrounding influences such as architecture, connections and functions. This irritation generates reaction: in regard of alternation and topography. The dynamic appearance of the park evolves from "fluent" parts that generate in sum a holistic scheme. Subareas of the park such as the "garden flux" or the "play flux" are understood in the characteristic of the overall concept.

Design Details:

The new park is situated in an agglomeration area of various fluxes: the motion lines cross and overlay each other, the traffic flows concentrate towards the central station, as well as the built environment in direction downtown.

Urban determined connections are transferred in park spanning textures, such as the frame. The basic theme of the design — the interpretation of the site as densification of various motions,

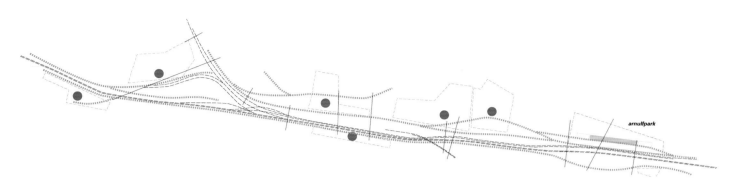

arnulfpark

flows and connections towards the city center is captured in the transformation of the typical train line accompanying woods in an urban grid planting structure. Starting from the west sparely interspersed trees concentrate while underlying a basic grid towards the eastern plaza to a dense grove. Interruptions and irritations are translated into sensitive shaped topography of the lawn areas opposing the rather plane urban surrounding.

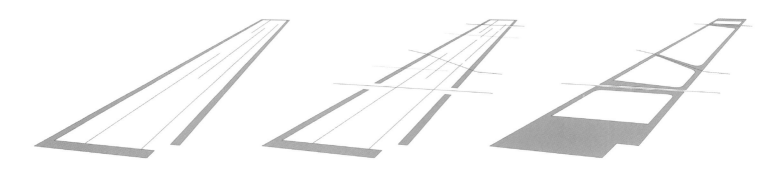

The dynamic appearance of the
park evolves from "fluent" parts
that generate in sum a holistic
scheme.

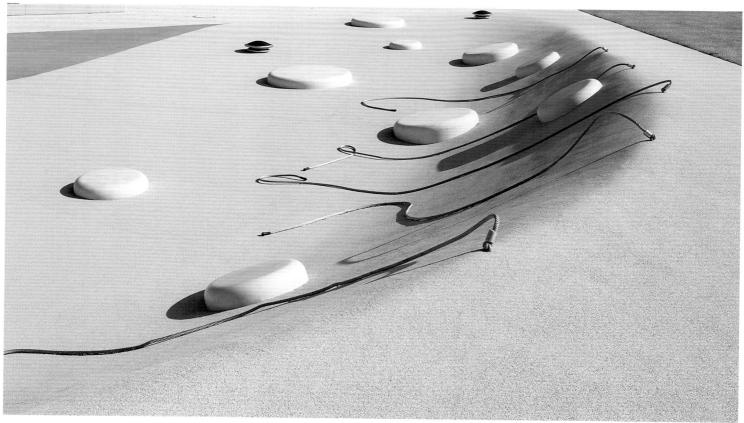

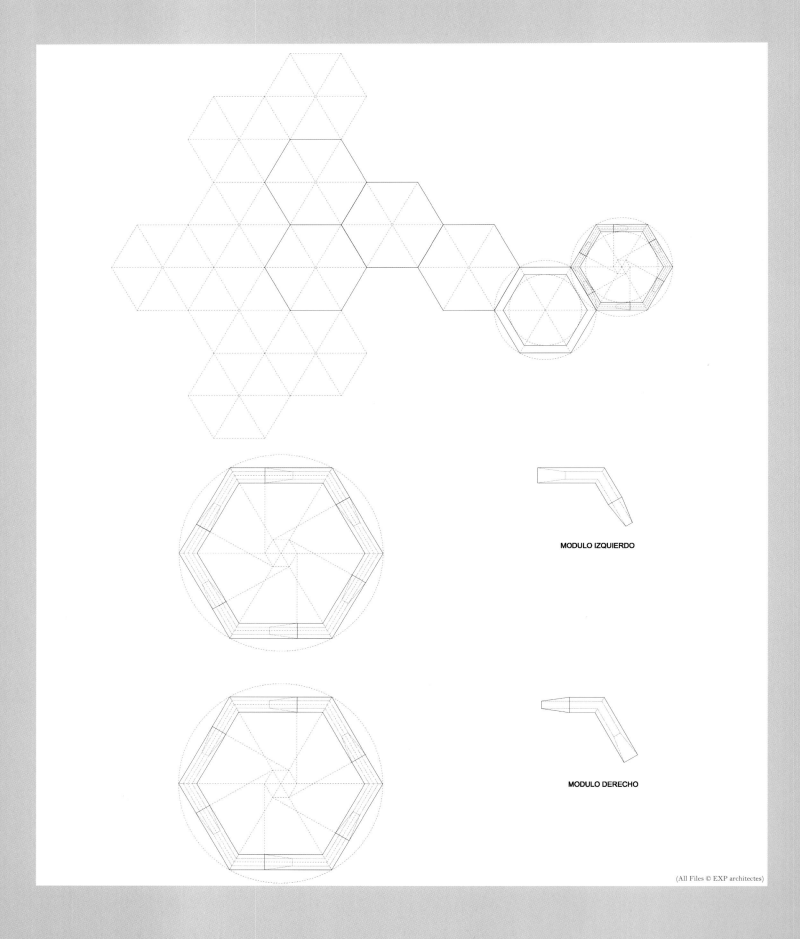

MODULO IZQUIERDO

MODULO DERECHO

Design Agency: EXP architectes

Photography: EXP architectes

Location: Valladolid, Spain

Area: 11, 000 m²

System of Modular Urban Furniture "Milenio"

General Description:

The initial objective of MILENIO was to offer a previously unprecedented piece of contemporary urban furniture, whose identity was strongly associated with the Plaza del Milenio in the city of Valladolid, Spain.

Design Concept:

The great variety of possible combinations permits the bench to find its place in an urban environment — city square, park, street, etc. — but also in a natural landscape, thus offering great freedom to architects and landscape designers.

Design Details:

Conceived from the geometric figure of the hexagon cut in 6 parts, the 2 modules — left and right — whose position can be singular or multiplied and reversible, have been supplemented by a straight module thus enhancing the propensity for multiple creative combinations.

Simply supported on the floor without anchoring, the benches were made of reinforced waterproof acid-etched concrete with stainless steel armatures. Glass micro balls are integrated into the mass, allowing natural or artificial light to glitter on the surface.

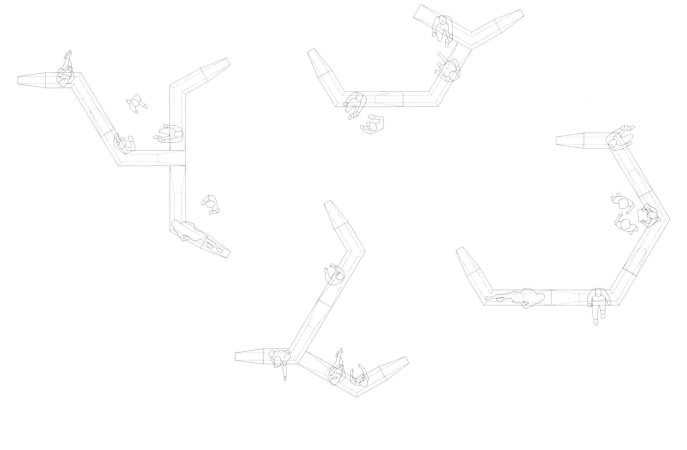

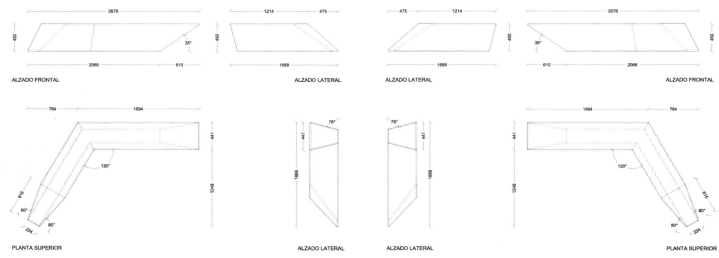

2678	1214	475	475	1214	2678
450					450
35°	450	450		35°	
2068	610	1689	1689	610	2068
ALZADO FRONTAL	ALZADO LATERAL	ALZADO LATERAL			ALZADO FRONTAL

PLANTA SUPERIOR 784 1894 441 120° 615 80° 80° 224 1248

441 76° 1689 ALZADO LATERAL

76° 441 1689 ALZADO LATERAL

1894 784 441 120° 615 80° 80° 224 1248 PLANTA SUPERIOR

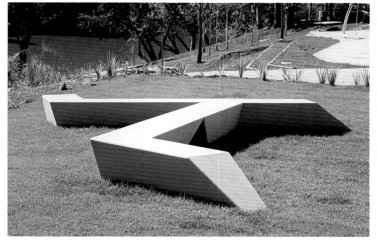

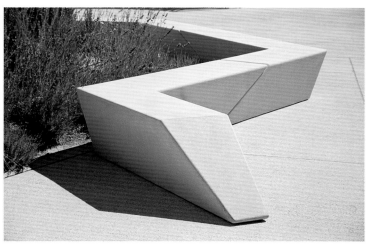

Design Agency: McGregor Coxall

Designer: Adrian McGregor, Christian Borchert

Photography: Christian Borchert

Location: Canberra, Australia

Area: 35, 000 m²

National Gallery of Australia

General Description:

The National Gallery of Australia (NGA) and its surrounding sculpture gardens were completed in 1983 and are located in the arts and civic campus of Australia's National Capital, Canberra. It has the largest collection of Australian indigenous art in the world, with over 7,500 works. Many of these are now prominently displayed in eleven new galleries.

PTW Architects were commissioned to extend the building and McGregor Coxall landscape architects were given the role of remaking the public realm and designing the new Australian Garden.

Design Concept:

The careful detailing of the new landscape aims to create a timeless and elegant public domain that relies on the patrons of the gallery and garden users to animate the space. The architect's intention was to make a very timeless contribution to the site, to add space, light and texture but without clutter. And one of the most wonderful aspects of the Australian National Gallery is that it continues to make an important contribution to the life of the city through its public space, both interior and exterior.

Design Details:

The new NGA and building extensions opened in October 2010. Influenced by the same book that Madigan referenced, "Space, Time and Architecture" by Siegfried Giedion, McGregor Coxall ensured the new landscape works embraced the geometric design

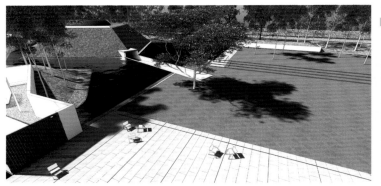

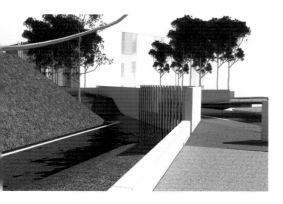

principles of the Madigan design by adopting the Golden Mean to proportion new elements. Extending the triangular grid of the original building created a framework for the location and arrangement of significant design elements such as pathways, bridges, walls and water elements.

The building and landscape were conceived at the outset to be tightly integrated so as to present a unified, legible, accessible public face to the NGA. Located on the previous car park, the main garden is designed around retained Eucalyptus trees. Two planar lawns form the main space creating an "inside-outside" room of huge proportions. The lawns are designed to host functions and events such as temporary art exhibitions and garden parties.

Visually, the center piece of the garden is a large pond into which the prominent sculpture "Within Without" by James Turrell appears to be sunken. Visitors descend down a ramp through the mirrored water surface of the pond to the interior where the monolithic nature of Turrell's work is evident. In the center of the sky space is a basalt stupa, a simple domed structure set within a water feature. Visitors move through the stupa to the carefully lit viewing chamber, or oculus, which opens to the sky above.

Sustainable design principles underpinning the project include the choice of low embodied energy materials. Australian slate and granite, concrete aggregates and gravel sourced in local quarries are consistent with the material palette of the existing works. Extensive indigenous planting local to the Canberra region is used to support the mature Eucalyptus trees to form a dense frame of bushland around the geometrically designed function lawns. Stormwater is harvested from all external areas and building roofs for internal reuse and for irrigation of the new garden.

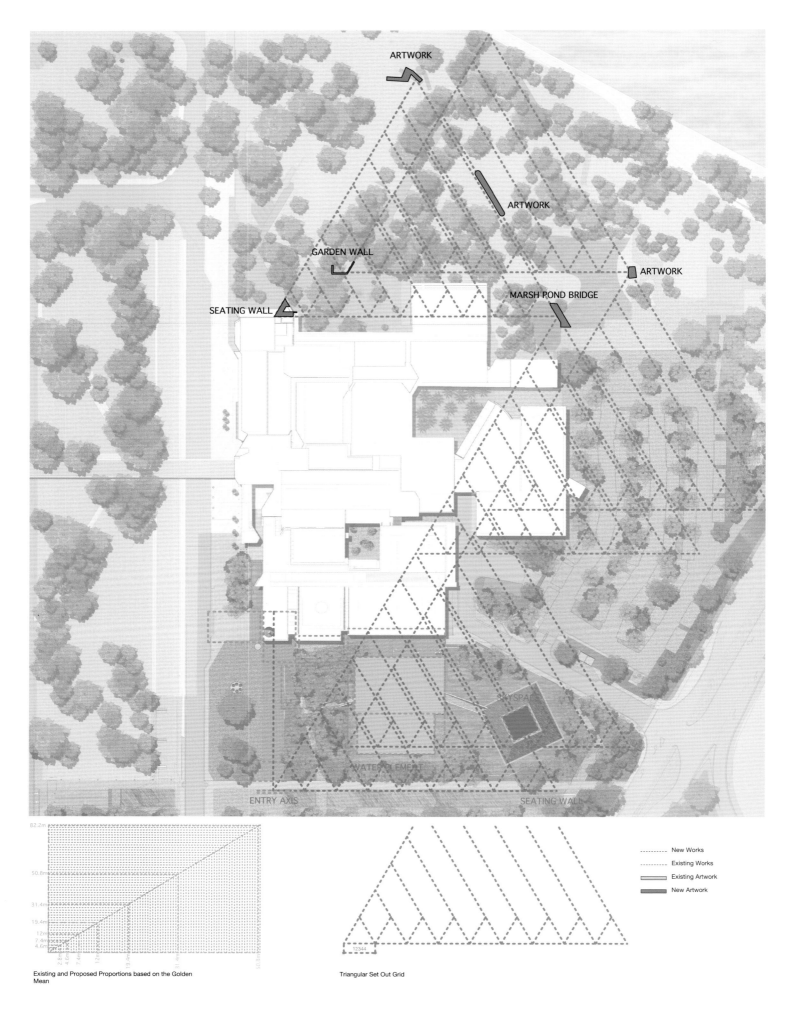

ARTWORK

ARTWORK

GARDEN WALL

ARTWORK

MARSH POND BRIDGE

SEATING WALL

SKYSPACE

WATER ELEMENT

ENTRY AXIS

SEATING WALL

82.2m
50.8m
31.4m
19.4m
12m
7.4m
4.6m

4.6m
7.4m
12m
19.4m
31.4m
50.8m

Existing and Proposed Proportions based on the Golden Mean

1 2 3 4 4

Triangular Set Out Grid

- - - - - New Works
- - - - - Existing Works
Existing Artwork
New Artwork

The careful detailing of the new landscape aims to create a timeless and elegant public domain that relies on the patrons of the gallery and garden users to animate the space.

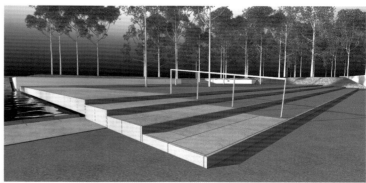

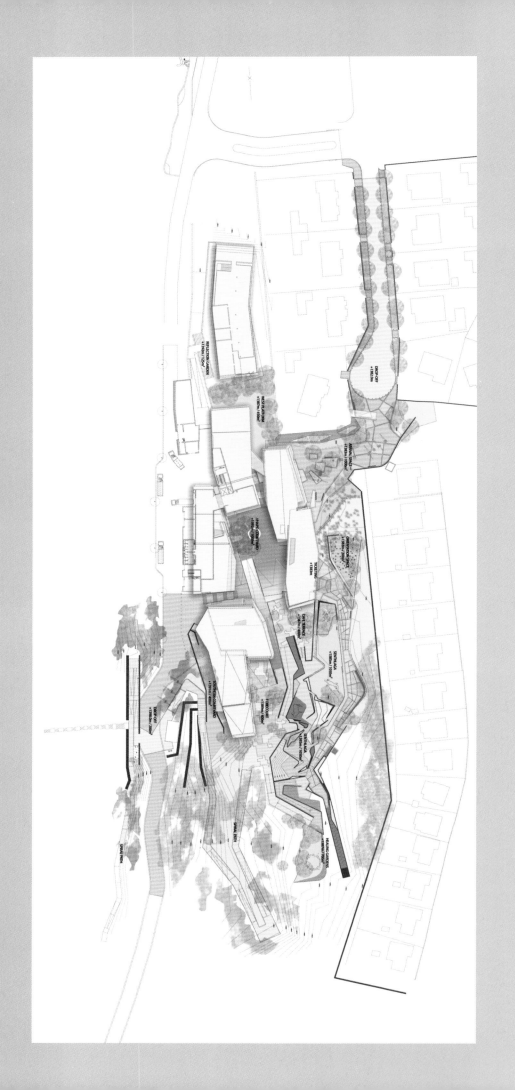

Design Agency: NBGM Landscape Architects, OCA Architects

Designer: Graham Young, Anton Comrie, Annamari Comrie, Andrew Kerrin

Photography: Graham Young, OCA Architects

Location: Tshwane, South Africa

Area: 400, 000 m²

Freedom Park

General Description:

Freedom Park is situated on Salvokop in Tshwane and fulfills the cultural role of Garden of Remembrance — a natural indigenous garden telling the story of South Africa's progression to freedom. It is intended as a natural symbol for reparation, a symbol of healing, a symbol of cleansing and a place where the souls of those who lost their lives in the quest for freedom can rest. It is also a place of pilgrimage, renewal and hope for all South Africans and even the whole mankind.

Design Concept:

Freedom Park was conceived as a narrative, a "journey to freedom" informed by traditional African culture and Indigenous Knowledge Systems (IKS) that have not been acknowledged through contemporary knowledge or records. The landscape design is also expressed by traditional forms, languages and principles of African architecture and space. Curved lines and rounded forms are typical elements. Natural and local materials were used as much as possible, and plants were transplanted to new locations to avoid construction footprints.

Design Details:

Five key elements — hapo, Isivivane, Sikumbuto, Moshate, and Tiva form the basis of this narrative and are linked by a wheelchair friendly pathway system that winds its way up the hill — all within the "Garden of Remembrance", which covers the entire hill.

Plants were carefully chosen to relate to the natural plant communities that occur across the site. They were also 'tested' by traditional healers for their appropriateness in use and location. Over 250 species of indigenous plants were used in the project.

Through rehabilitation and conservation, the landscape intervention heals the original scars of the site and symbolically, of history. As the new planting grows in, the architectural elements of Freedom Park will look as though they emerge out of the hill and are one with it — like much of historic African interventions such as Great Zimbabwe and Thulamela. All exotic trees were removed (or are being removed) from the site, and invasive species are being eliminated over time through management. Rare species were grown at an on-site nursery established specifically for the project to establish a landscape that offers a much broader ecology than what the original site had to offer. New indigenous species were used in a bold, dramatic and pragmatic way — a symbolic healing of the landscape through human expression.

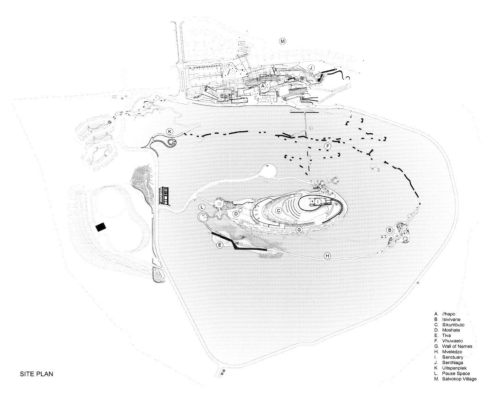

SITE PLAN

A. //hapo
B. Isivivane
C. Sikumbuto
D. Moshate
E. Tiva
F. Vhuwaelo
G. Wall of Names
H. Mveledzo
I. Sanctuary
J. Senthlaga
K. Uitspanplek
L. Pause Space
M. Salvokop Village

The reeds are the project's main iconic component. They constitute a transparent element encircling the top of the hill and the Wall of Names, drawing a line against the horizon while maintaining the visual outline of the hilltop.

The reeds are actually stainless steel "masts" that range in height from 1meter to 34meters. The challenge was the need to consider the relationships of these sculptures to the landscape, the project's content and the visual manifestation of "monument". The reeds are perhaps the element of the project that most epitomizes the opportunity and restrictions inherent in the blurring of landscape, art and architecture.

93

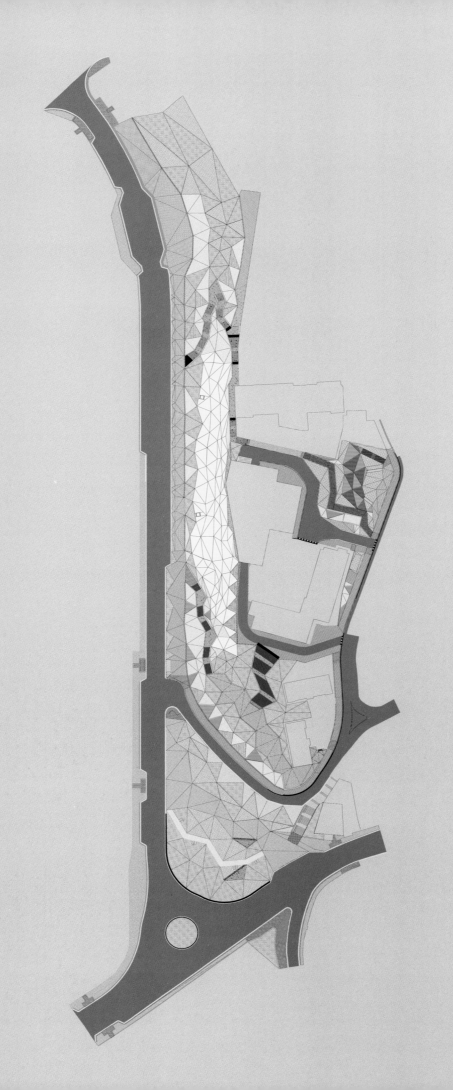

Design Agency: ACXT Architects

Designer: César Azcárate, Ana Morón

Photography: Aitor Ortiz

Location: Bilbao, Spain

Area: 1, 000 m²

Galindez Slope and Pau Casals Square

General Description:

This project consisted of a rocky embankment with a difference in level of 18 meters, with stability problems that caused continuous landslides , creating a physical barrier between two districts communicated only by a small, poorly-maintained metal stairway, which represented a social barrier, isolating the district of Otxarcoaga,

with its severe integration problems, from the rest of the city. The aim of the project is to consolidate the embankment and recover this derelict area, which acts like a physical barrier and disintegrating element in the city.

Design Concept:

To shape the embankment by using inclined planes of different materials reveals their strange topography to the city. The triangular planes are formed by different materials: the existing rock, vegetation of different colors, concrete in those areas which required consolidation and light, reconstructing their silhouette at night.

To create connecting elements between the top and bottom levels lessens the impact of the embankment as a physical barrier in the city. To create a horizontal platform takes advantage of the height of this area.

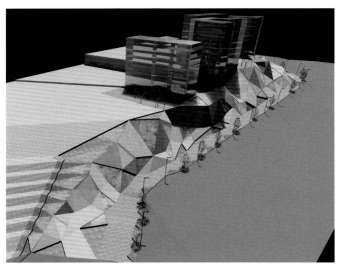

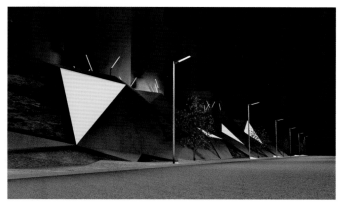

Design Details:

All the elements in the project form part of this recreated topography: the stairways, the sitting areas, the public toilets. All these elements are included within a single fold. Following the embankment project, the architects were commissioned to develop the Plaza de Pau Casals project and create a children's play area over a former electricity substation. All these locations are situated on steep slopes next to the embankment.

It has been necessary to treat these spaces in accordance with the rules of geometry. The architects continue using triangular planes.

In the children's playing area the planes are soft — of grass, rubber, flowers. There are built-in toboggans. The old substation is enveloped in a fold of wooden slabs that convert it into part of the topography.

In the Plaza de Pau Casals, the folds envelop a retaining wall and generate a space edged by gentle slopes where formerly there had been a crossroads, planting planes between the existing trees in the old central reserve, planes of colored concrete and planes of water to sit next to.

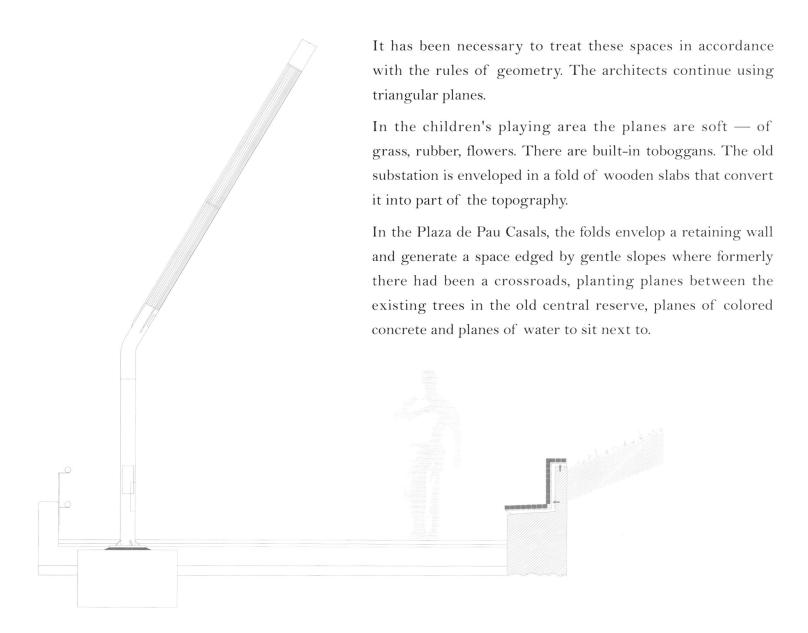

The triangular planes are
formed by different materials:
the existing rock, vegetation
of different colours, concrete
in those areas which
required consolidation and
light, reconstructing their
silhouette at night.

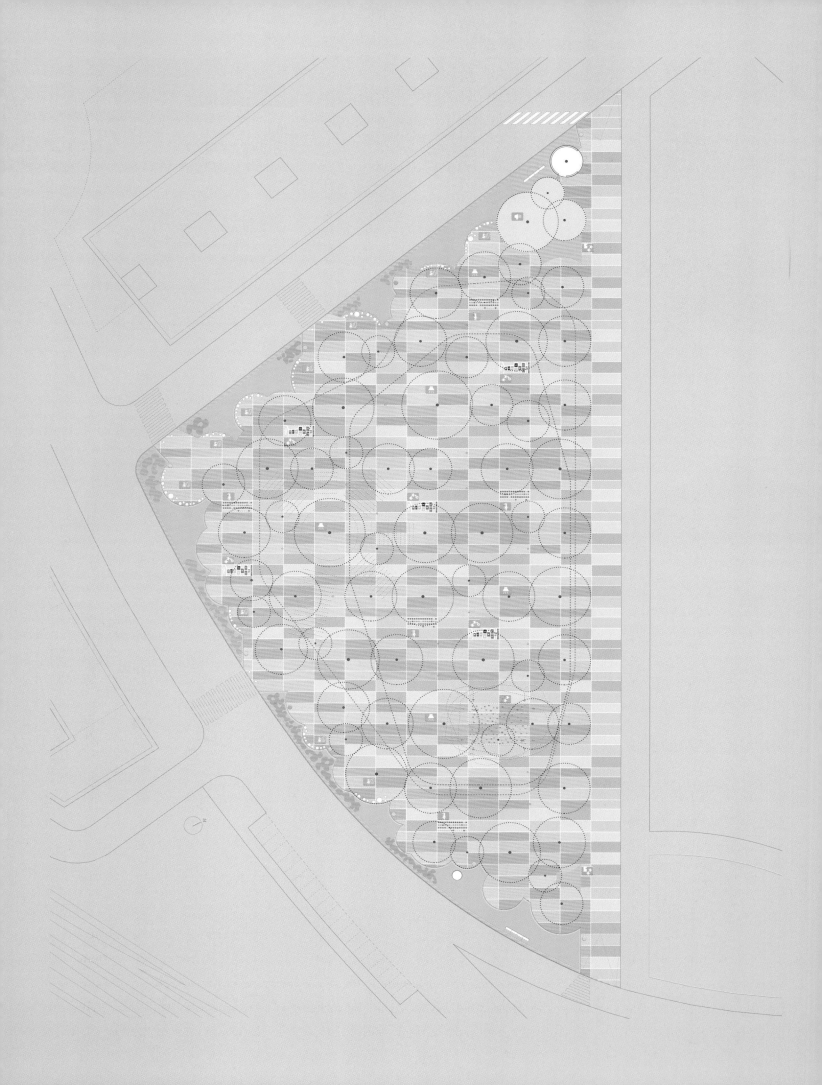

Design Agency: Paredes Pino

Designer: Fernando G. Pino, Manuel G. de Paredes

Photography: Paredes Pino

Location: Córdoba, Spain

Area: 11, 920 m²

Open Center for Civic Activities

General Description:

Open Center for Civic Activities (CAAC) is treated like a huge board game that can hold any kind of activities such as a temporary market.

Design Concept:

CAAC is projected by a solution based on prefabricated circular elements that vary in height and diameter and arranged in a flexible but tight way, allowing a view similar to the shadows of an urban forest.

Design Details:

The structure of the project is made up of steel umbrellas. The treatment of the bottom surface is reflective, giving the place a huge potential in the way that light activates the color by reflection.

The design of the plant cover is closely connected to other points of view, from which the action is perceived. Therefore, the treatment of surface color on top is of great importance.

The cover is composed of parasols with diameters between 7 and 15 meters. In turn, the heights are also variable between 4 and 7 meters. This allows great flexibility with little variability and constructive elements. Furthermore, with the position at different heights, it avoids excessive opacity of construction, and allows the passage of light reflection through the various umbrellas. Artificial lighting is fixed in the same parts, relying on a uniform light on the ground plane and the capture of light by reflection from the undersides of the parasols.

The display and
application of the
steel umbrella
structure allow
the light to go
through and the
free integration
of colors, making
this project one of
a kind.

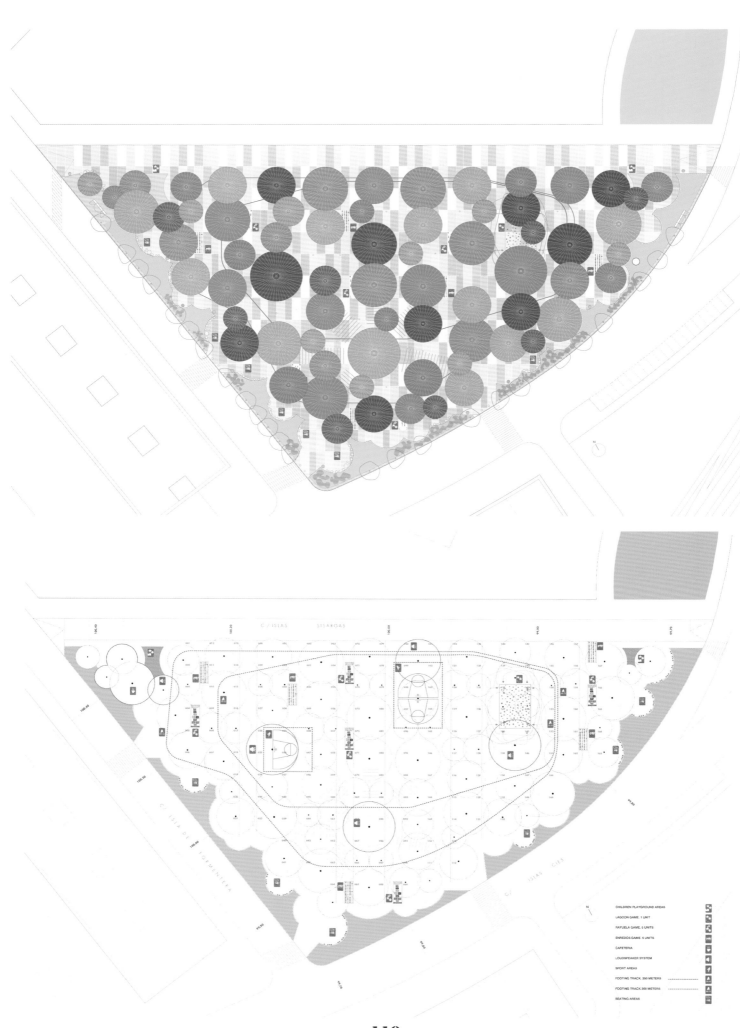

CHILDREN PLAYGROUND AREAS

LAGOON GAME. 1 UNIT

RAYUELA GAME. 5 UNITS

ENREDOS GAME. 5 UNITS

CAFETERIA

LOUDSPEAKER SYSTEM

SPORT AREAS

FOOTING TRACK. 250 METERS

FOOTING TRACK. 300 METERS

SEATING AREAS

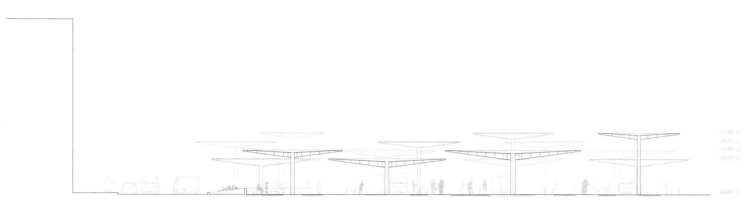

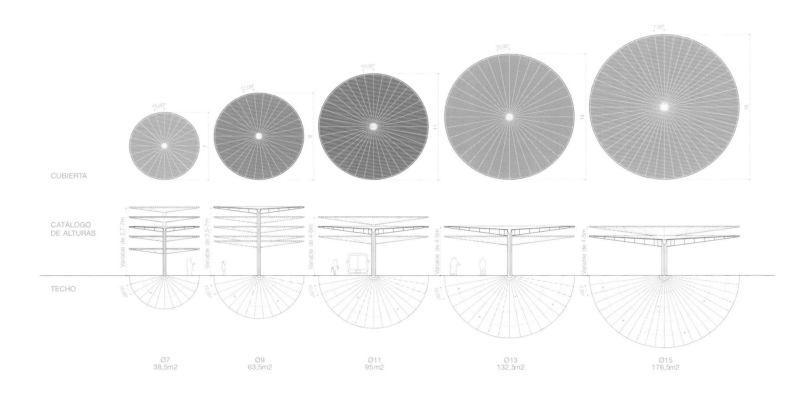

CUBIERTA

CATÁLOGO
DE ALTURAS

TECHO

Ø7	Ø9	Ø11	Ø13	Ø15
38,5m2	63,5m2	95m2	132,5m2	176,5m2

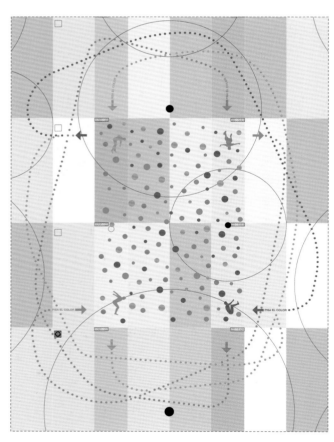

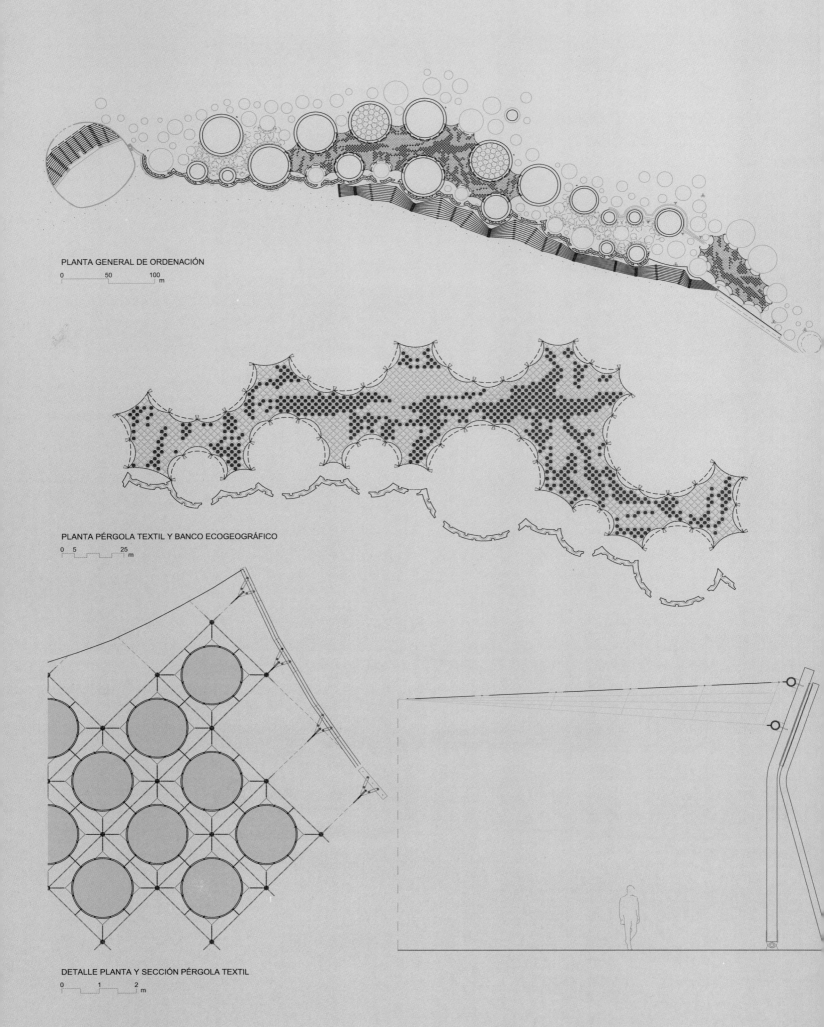

PLANTA GENERAL DE ORDENACIÓN

0   50   100
              m

PLANTA PÉRGOLA TEXTIL Y BANCO ECOGEOGRÁFICO

0 5   25
              m

DETALLE PLANTA Y SECCIÓN PÉRGOLA TEXTIL

0   1   2 m

Design Agency: BATLLE I ROIG ARCHITECTS

Designer: Enric Batlle, Joan Roig

Photography: Eva Serrats

Location: Zaragoza, Spain

Area: 140, 000 m²

114-119

The Riverfront and Thematic Squares

General Description:

The specific project drafted for the Expo Zaragoza 2008 developed the arrangement of this lower platform, the river front, the thematic squares where these ephemeral pavilions would sit, the outdoor auditorium and the large public space that linked all of these activities.

Design Concept:

The project was conceived as a "garden of water drops" consisting of a sequence of circular spaces intended not only for the various pavilions but also for other uses that gave meaning to them after the end of the event, from small groves to ponds or recreational squares.

Design Details:

This plan arranged to divide the precinct into two platforms at different levels that were being developed in parallel to the river. The upper one, which would

contain the main pavilions, was at city level, while the lower one, which was located in seasonally flooded areas, connected with the river promenade running along the left bank of the River Ebro. This platform would contain the thematic pavilions, which would be dismantled after the exposition.

Much of the interstitial space between the circles was covered with a stretched textile pergola over 10,000m² of surface, supported by metal pillars. Its design was specifically created to try to reduce the temperature of the itinerary in more than 10°. In order to achieve this, the architects used a special fabric and arranged it in large circular pieces alternating sunny and shadowy areas as not to enclose the place completely.

The river front was treated as an amphitheater on the River from which one could view the night shows at the Expo. By using wood planks, the architects designed topography with references to the rising of the River Ebro, making its use compatible between a public space and its sporadic hydraulic activity. A large bench along the river perimeter, the most important geographical location in the exhibition, was placed between both spaces. In the project, this 700-meter-long bench was called "ecogeographic".

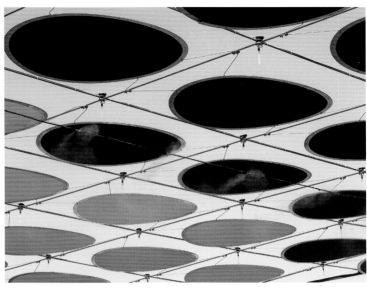

Design Agency: ASPECT Studios

Photography: Andrew Lloyd

Location: Elwood, Australia

Area: 21,000 m²

Elwood Foreshore

General Description:

The urban coastal promenade and beach of Elwood foreshore is part of the highly popular coastline destination of Melbourne's Port Phillip Bay, and is 8 km south from the city's central business district. The redevelopment of Elwood foreshore was driven by the need to restore quality to a public open space by rethinking its form and function in structural terms. And the design gives back to the community an open and inviting foreshore place that provides for a range of activities from quiet enjoyment to large scale, surf lifesaving competitions.

Design Concept:

The new beach promenade orchestrates pedestrian and cycle movement, stepped access to the beach, view lines, and provides a rhythmic series of platforms for beachside activities. It demonstrates that a seamless connection can be made between functional design and design elegance.

Design Details:

The primary, horizontal relationships between the foreshore public spaces and the beach and sea were dislocated. Re-design asserted the rightful dominance of the strong horizontal elements of the landscape — the seating wall and its lighting, other low concrete walls, the flat grass area, the "sunbathing" platforms and plaza edge, and low indigenous coastal vegetation. The only vertical elements in the landscape are the pole lighting, showers and canopy trees.

Car parking was too close to the primary attraction — the foreshore — and conflicted with pedestrian and cyclist movement through the site, affected views out to the water, and the main entrance road separated the car park from the foreshore. Re-design inverted these relationships and ensured all through traffic was kept as far as possible from the main pubic entrance.

The space was poorly organized, drainage insufficient, and few trees provided good and well-situated shade. Creating clarity of space and usability were essential. The integration and spatial requirements of the numerous facilities occupying the site — the Surf Life Saving Club, Sailing Club, Angling Club, restaurant, café, car park, and Tennis Club — and their relationships to the surrounding parkland were all considered throughout the restructuring of the site. Also, the foreshore design ensures capacity for large scale events such as the swimming carnivals.

Changes to the traffic system gave back usable public land to the foreshore. Shared paths were created to reduce conflict between bicycles, pedestrians and motor vehicles and to ensure safety and accessibility. A new regional cycle way and beach promenade were integrated into the design.

Recycled asphalt was used for pavements to car parks, and existing subgrades recycled into paths wherever possible. Extensive and entirely indigenous plantings sought to restore and protect elements of the sensitive bay environment.

The new beach promenade orchestrates pedestrian and cycle movement, stepped access to the beach, view lines, and provides a rhythmic series of platforms for beachside activities. It demonstrates that a seamless connection can be made between functional design and design elegance.

Design Agency: *Claude Cormier + Associés inc.*

Designer: *Claude Cormier*

Photography: *Claude Cormier + Associés inc.*

Eastern Construction, Waterfront Toronto, Jesse Colin Jackson

Location: *Toronto, Canada*

Area: *8, 500 m²*

Sugar Beach

General Description:

Located at the foot of Lower Jarvis Street adjacent to the Redpath Sugar Factory, Sugar Beach is the first public space visitors see as they travel along Queens Quay from the central waterfront. It is the second urban beach proposed for Toronto's downtown waterfront, and the latest addition to the amber necklace of Toronto's lakefront beachscape. It is a sequel to HtO, the waterfront's first beach park.

Design Concept:

The design for Sugar Beach draws upon the industrial heritage of the area and its relationship to the neighboring Redpath Sugar factory. With the fragrance of sugar in the air, the park's conceptual reference is experienced in both sight and smell. And sugar as a concept was used to establish a language for many of the elements throughout the park.

Design Details:

The beach allows visitors to enjoy the afternoon as they read, play in the sand or watch boats on the lake. A dynamic water feature embedded into a granite maple leaf beside the beach makes cooling off fun for adults and children. This interactive fountain transitions into a spectacle of illuminated choreography at night.

©Claude Cormier + Associés inc.

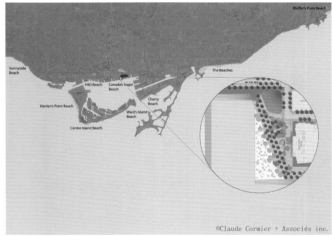

©Claude Cormier + Associés inc.

The park's plaza offers a dynamic space for public events. One of the park's granite rock outcropping and three grass mounds give the public an amphitheater for outdoor concerts on the stage of the adjacent entertainment studio, as well as unique vantage points in the spaces between the mounds for smaller events.

Between the plaza and the beach, people stroll through the park along a promenade which features granite cobblestones in a maple leaf mosaic pattern. Lined with maple trees, the promenade offers a shaded route to the water's edge providing the public with many opportunities along the way to sit and enjoy views to the lake, beach or plaza. Situated under the promenade is a generous system of silva cells that provide over 30 m³ of soil for each tree. This, along with the large soil volumes in the berms and under the sand, will ensure that the maples, weeping willows, and white pines at Sugar Beach will be able to grow to their full potential.

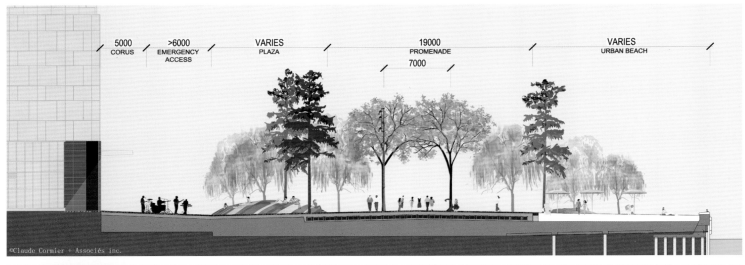

©Waterfront Toronto

©Waterfront Toronto

Jesse Colin Jackson

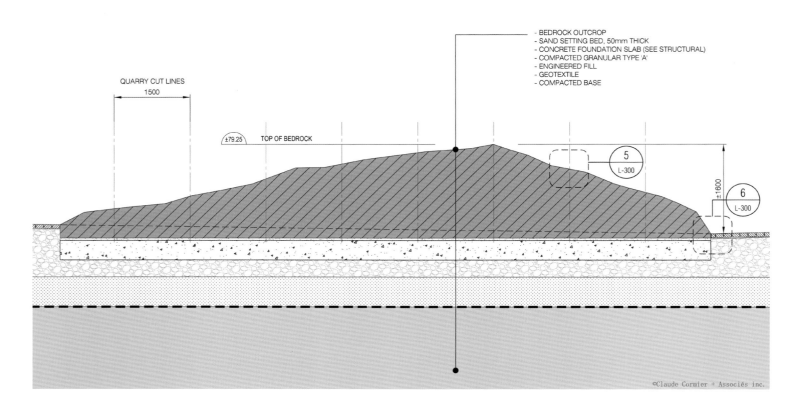

QUARRY CUT LINES
1500

±79.25 TOP OF BEDROCK

- BEDROCK OUTCROP
- SAND SETTING BED, 50mm THICK
- CONCRETE FOUNDATION SLAB (SEE STRUCTURAL)
- COMPACTED GRANULAR TYPE 'A'
- ENGINEERED FILL
- GEOTEXTILE
- COMPACTED BASE

5
L-300

±1600

6
L-300

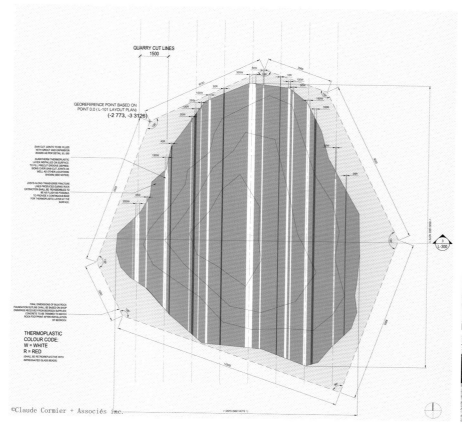

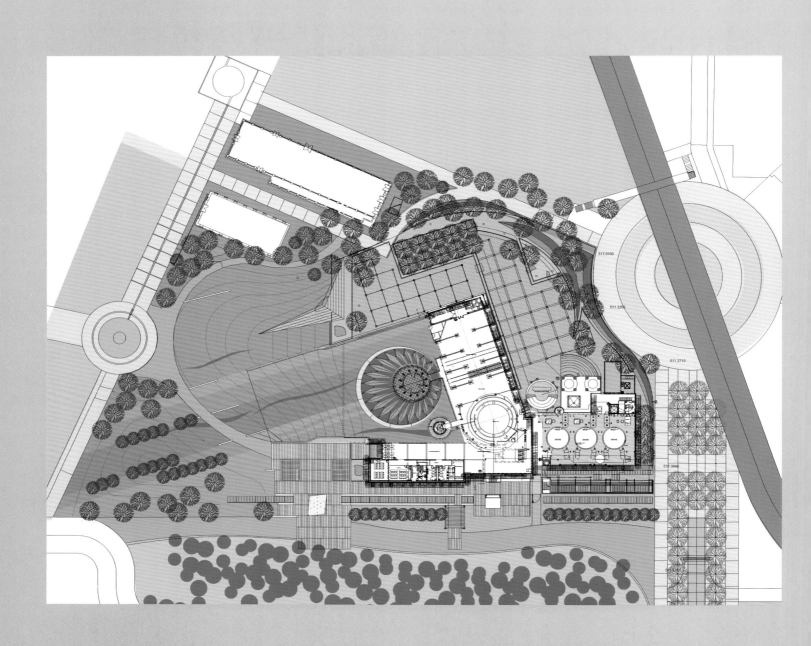

Design Agency: *Surfacedesign, Inc.*	Location: *Monterrey, Mexico*
Designer: *James A. Lord, Claudia Harari*	Area: *15, 000 m²*
Photography: *Paul Riveria/Archphoto,*	
Abigail Guzman Tamex/Grafix, James Lord	

Museo del Acero Horno³

General Description:

In 1986, the city of Monterrey, Mexico reclaimed an expansive 1.5 hectare brownfield site of a former steel production facility. Eleven years later, the site's decommissioned blast furnace has emerged as the Museo del Acero Horno³, the Museum of Steel, which serves as a new focal point for the region.

Design Concept:

The Museo del Acero Horno³ narrates the story of steel production both to the generations who remember the history of the site and to younger visitors who may be unaware of the region's legacy. Principals of sustainability are at the core of the landscape design of the Museo del Acero Horno³.

Design Details:

The overall landscape design emphasizes the physical profile of the 70-meter furnace structure while complementing the modern design of the new structures. The history of steel is an important narrative element throughout the site, and thus steel, much of it reclaimed from the site (such as the ore-embedded steel rails used to define the outdoor exhibit spaces) is used extensively to help define public plazas and delineate fountains and landscaped terraces. Large, free-formed steel objects and machinery unearthed during excavation were incorporated as stepping stones and other features. The design approach melds industrial site reclamation — and the adaptive re-use of on-

site materials — with ecological restoration through the use of green technologies.

All of the storm water runoff within the site's boundaries is treated in a series of on-site treatment runnels. These surround the exhibition areas and reinterpret the former industrial canals that once moved steel production by-products within the site. Aquatic plants and wetland macrophytes bio-remediate and treat storm water before it enters an underground cistern where it is stored for dry season irrigation.

Two water features are integral to the narrative of the project, while helping to define and locate the public space adjacent to the museum. In the main esplanade, the steel plates that formerly clad the exterior of the main hall were repurposed into a stepped canal over which water cascades. The 200-meter-long feature alludes to the tracks used daily to train in the thousands of tons of raw materials that were off-loaded in this location, and serves as a visual connection to the rain garden in the landscape beyond. At the museum's entrance, the stepped canal culminates in the misting fountain, a grid of rocks visibly embedded with ore. This trompe l'oeil evokes the caustic heating process once used to extract ore, but instead of steam it generates a cooling mist that blows over the plaza — a pleasant surprise for visitors in Monterrey's hot and arid climate.

The use of green roofs (extensive and intensive) over the museum which comprises the largest such roof system in Latin America helps to reduce the visual impact of the new buildings. The existing furnace rises from this newly created ground plane. On the higher roof, a variety of drought-tolerant sedums have been arranged according to the structural roof patterns of the new architecture, and are contained by what appears to be a floating steel disk. A circular viewing deck allows visitors to take in the expanse of surrounding regional landscape, including the distant Sierra Madres, which are echoed in the roof's mounded shape. Below, Alfombra verde (green blanket) a less constrained meadow of tall grasses — an abstraction of the native landscape — creates a connection to the landscape's pre-industrial context both functioning as a bioremediation for degraded soil and increasing thermal benefits for the new structure.

By thoughtfully repurposing found industrial artifacts and incorporating new green technologies that work in concert with the architecture and the greater landscape, the designers have created an outdoor exhibition space that interprets the area's historic uses while celebrating artistic opportunities for the future.

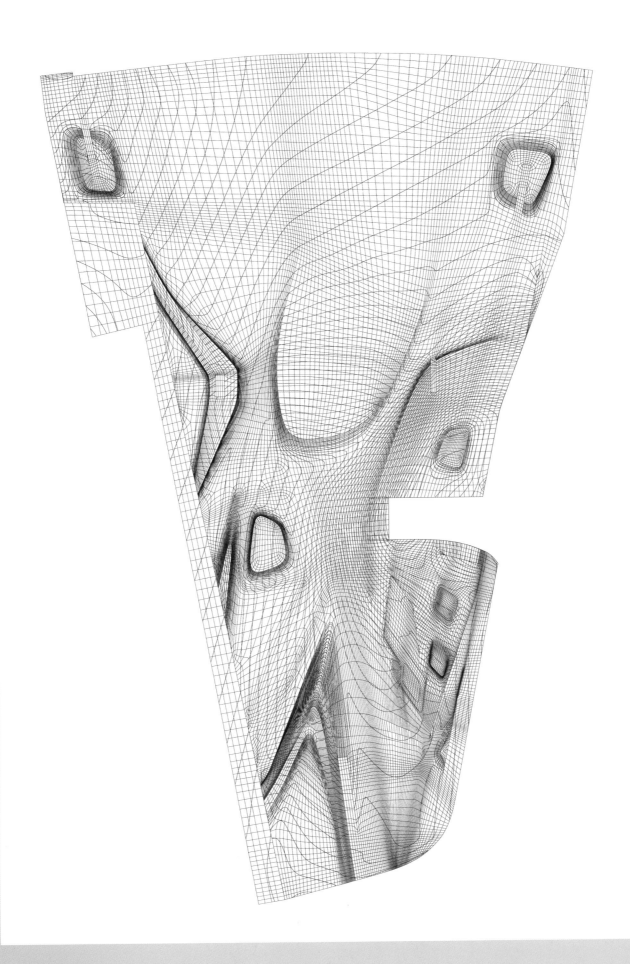

Design Agency: *LAAC Architects*

Photography: *Günter Richard Wett*

Location: *Innsbruck, Austria*

Area: *9, 000 m²*

New Design for Eduard-Wallnöfer-Platz

General Description:

Eduard-Wallnöfer-Platz was the largest but neglected public square in the center of the city of Innsbruck in Tyrol, Austria. The site nevertheless keeps a symbolic significance with the four memorials positioned there.

Design Concept:

Goal of the intervention at Eduard-Wallnöfer-Platz (Landhausplatz) was to create a contemporary urban public space that negotiates between the various contradictory conditions and constraints of the site and establishes a stage for a new mélange of urban activities characterized by a wide range of diversity. It also aims to compensate for existing misconceptions and to reinforce the monument's historical significance.

©Günter Richard Wett

Design Details:

The bright surface of the square functions as a three-dimensional projection field on which the protagonists together with the trees cause a high-contrast dynamic play of light and shadow during daytime. In front of this background the seasons are staged powerfully. Indirect light reflected from the floor sculpture directs the scenery at night times.

In the northern part of the square, the spacious flat area in front of the Landhaus is conceived as a generous multi-purpose event space providing the according infrastructure. A large scale fountain activates the expanded field and provides cooling-down in summertime.

South of the liberation monument the topography features a variety of spatial situations for manifold

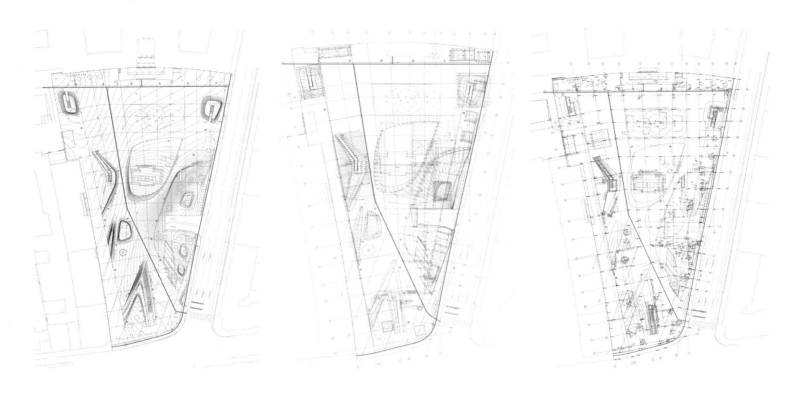

©Günter Richard Wett

utilizations. The texture of the concrete surface varies according the type of geometrical configuration. Beneath many trees the floor continuously merges into seat accommodations with a terrazzo-like polished finish.

The sculpture group of one of the monuments is integrated into the basin of a new fountain where water runs down steps cut into a slope.

The shoal fountain and the water games in front of the Landhaus provide playground for children and cool down the climate in summer locally. There are drinking fountains in different heights for children and adults.

The surface of the square is realized in modulated slabs out of in-situ concrete, joined by bolts that deal with shearing forces. Infrastructural elements for the organization of events which can take place anywhere on the square are integrated in the construction of slab-fields of max.100 square meter.

Drainage of the whole square including the fountains is located completely at the open joints between the individual fields so that there is no drainage pit visible on the whole site. An innovative buffer system allows that — despite of the existence of a subterranean garage — all the appearing surface water drains away within the property.

©Günter Richard Wett

©Günter Richard Wett

©Günter Richard Wett

143

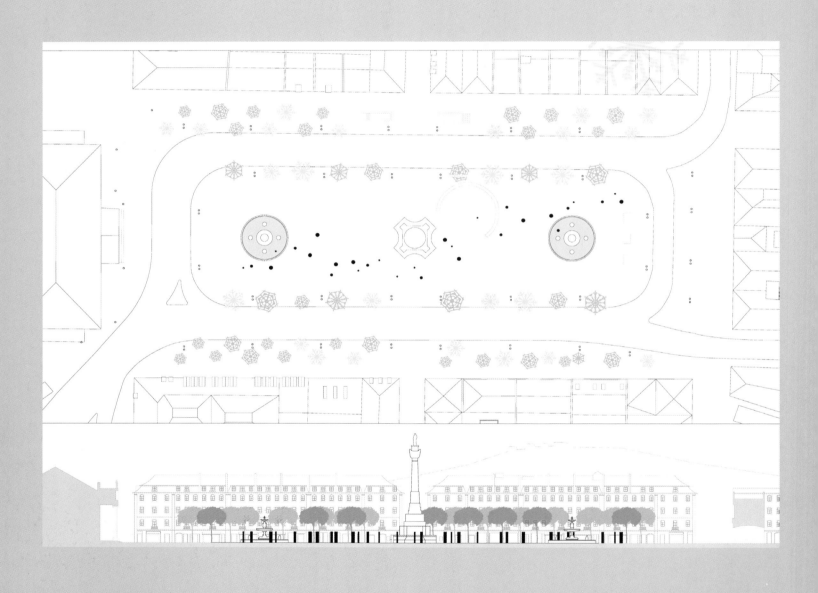

Design Agency: *LIKEarchitects*

Designer: *Diogo Aguiar, Teresa Otto*

Photography: *FG+SG Architectural Photography,*
Dinis Sottomayor

Location: *Lisbon, Portugal*

Area: *40 m²*

Frozen Trees

General Description:

"Frozen Trees" is a temporary installation for Christmas lighting in D. Pedro IV square in Lisbon. An illuminated, frozen and fractal Christmas landscape that affects and alters the path of passersby was built.

Design Concept:

Designed from the creative association of "Rationell Variera" piece by K Hagberg/M Hagberg (IKEA – 1.5€), and taking advantage from its shape, "Frozen Trees" brings a domestic object to the scale of the town — thus dissociating it from its original function and leading to the loss of its identity as a single element, making a general call for creativity in the current socio-economic conjecture.

Design Details:

The volumes, made of multiple holes, are visually trespassed and define an ethereal presence in the square. The installation takes then advantage from the holes of the original object and the translucent properties of its material — polypropylene plastic — simultaneously flexible, non-inflammable and highly absorbent and potentiating the transmittance of light, either natural or artificial. Blending with the urban surrounding, "Frozen Trees" presents different characteristics day and night: by day, the trees make surprising shadows and the ensemble makes an abstract, white and tracery landscape, through which we see the surrounding; by night, illuminated from inside by LEDs, the elements, as street lamps, explode with white light, creating a Christmas ambience with variable intensity.

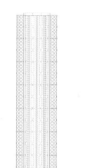
3.6m
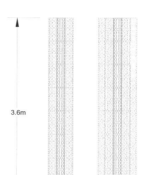

Structural and Constructive Strategy

A 160 x 450 mm plastic piece is the basic element for the modular logic of this project; in fact, it is the size of the element that draws the structural module.

Each of the 30 trees is the same height — 3.6 meters — but three different diameters coexist — 5, 10 or 15 pieces in the bottom — totalling ten units on each of the three sizes.

The light metal structure is made of vertical profiles and horizontal triangular rings; the first receive the IKEA pieces, the latter the illumination network made of monochromatic LEDs.

Twenty four hundred "Rationell Variera" pieces were previously fastened to the structures, still at the studio, and later transported to the Rossio. Once at the destination, the basis of these elements was fixed to the ground, to ensure its stability.

Sustainability Strategy

"Frozen Trees" is a fast production and easy set-up installation, able to pop-up and disappear from a city without destroying or damaging anything. "Frozen Trees" illumination is based upon a white monochromatic LED system, characterized by low voltage and energy consumption and also able to adjust the light's intensity. Each element's energy supply is made by a car battery that ensures its autonomy throughout the Christmas period. Regarding the effect/cost ratio, choosing a standard object is proved to be an effective solution, allowing for a unique aesthetic result for a very competitive price. On the other hand, polypropylene plastic pieces are reusable and highly recyclable.

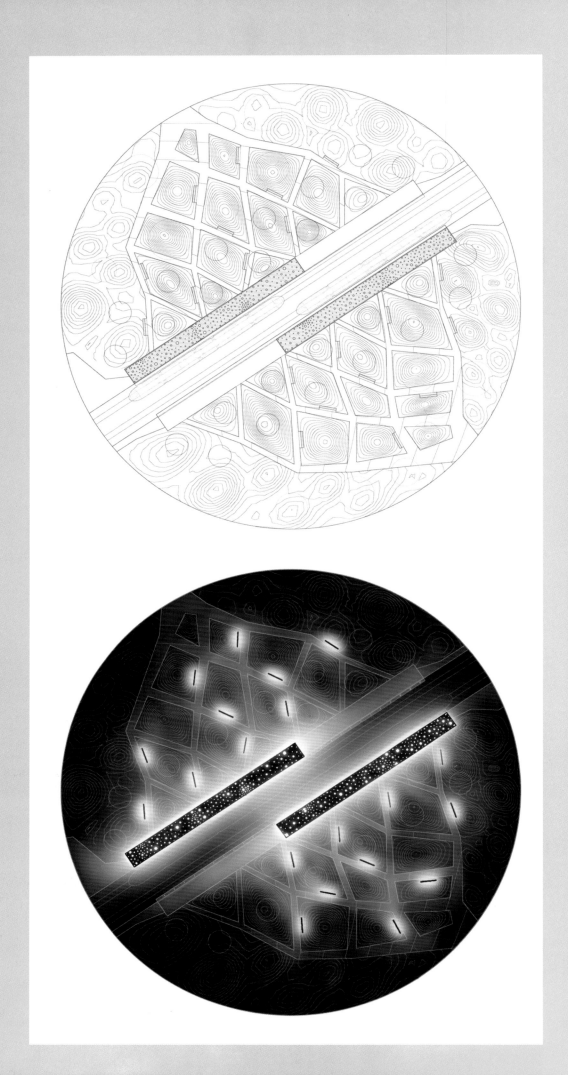

Design Agency: Subarquitectura

Designer: Andrés Silanes, Fernando Valderrama, Carlos Bañón

Photography: David Frutos, Subarquitectura, Alberto
Vicente Mayo

Location: Alicante, Spain

Area: 5, 090 m²

Tram Stop

©Alberto Vicente Mayo

©SUBARQUITECTURA

General Description:

Alicante is a city with a population of 400,000 in the southeast Mediterranean Spanish coast. Over the last years, there has been building a new tram infrastructure, using the old rails of the local train. This stop is the central stage of a new line of the tram, which links the center of the city to the residential areas of San Juan beach.

Design Concept:

The construction of the Tram Stop was the opportunity to bring back a stolen space to the city: to turn a traffic circle into a public space.

Design Details:

Through a fractal access system deformed in each side to avoid the existing trees, the travelers can arrive in a frontal way to the platform in 32 different possibilities.

Over the platforms, 2 empty boxes (36 m long, 3 m wide, 2.5 m high) create a floating void slightly over the travelers' heads. It matches the size of the train, creating an intermediate scale between buildings and urban elements.

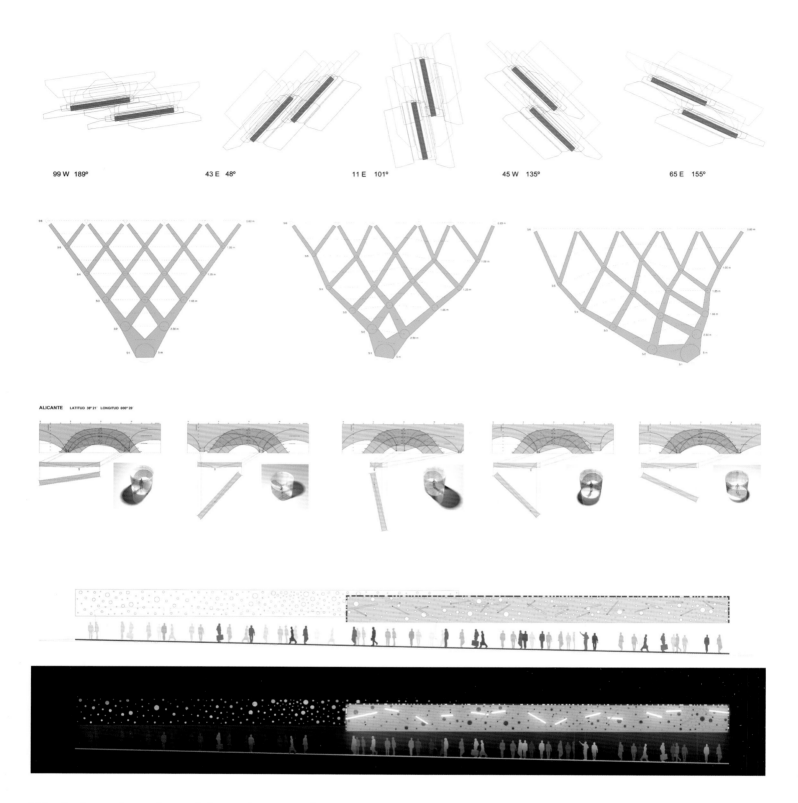

The holes reduce the weight as increase the resistance to normal tensions, and equally decrease wind pressures among the surfaces. Benches are spread over the garden close to the vegetation and the paths, creating a public place overlaying the quiet of the seated people and the movement of the people walking. Light and air pass through, smoothing the shadow and generating a soft breeze in summer months. At night the boxes are transformed into two giant lamps. There is no difference between structure and envelope, neither between roof and walls. It is an isotropic material in both conception and construction.

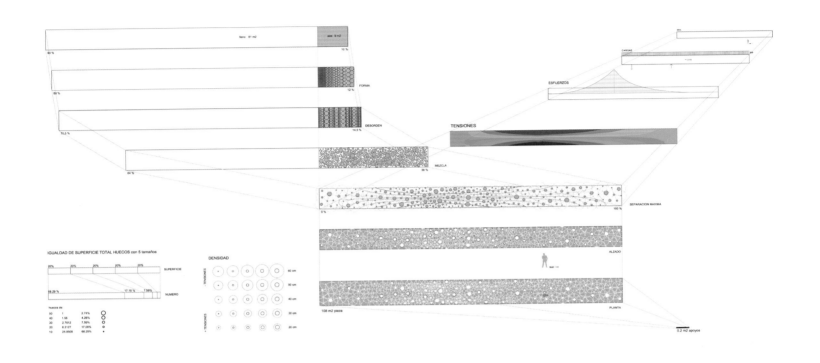

IGUALDAD DE SUPERFICIE TOTAL HUECOS con 5 tamaños

©David Frutos

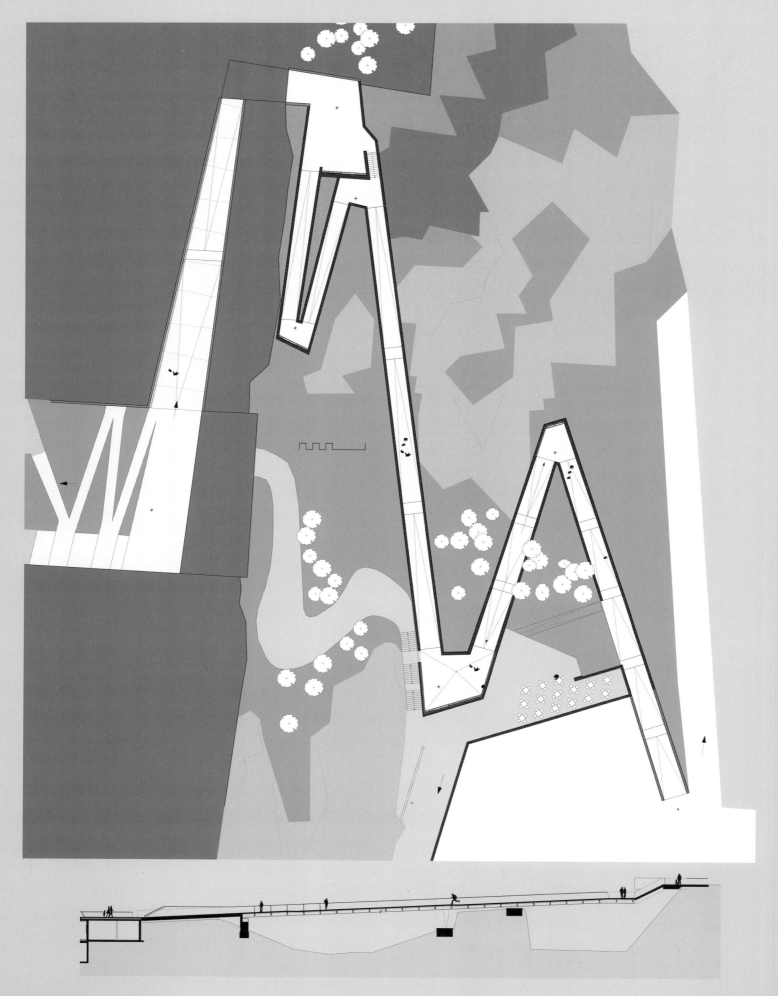

M. 1:200

Design Agency: AllesWirdGut Architektur

Creative Director: AllesWirdGut

Photography: Hertha Hurnaus, Petra Schneidhofer

Location: St. Magarethen, Austria

Area: 5, 580 m²

Redesign of the Roman Quarry Disposed Opera Festivals

© Hertha Hurnaus

General Description:

A show in the Roman quarry doubtless is a unique experience for every visitor, whether it is the classical-music lover enjoying a performance of the opera festival or a local watching the annual passion play with his friends as amateur actors.

Design Concept:

The basic idea of the design is to extend the ambience of the magnificent rock-face scenery to all parts of the theatrical arena so as to make it a more palpable and visual enveloping experience.

©Petra Schneidhofer

Design Details:

The playing and singing under the open sky on a gentle summer night, far away from the noise of the street is an experience that even the average visitor who is not too much into opera and passion plays will find overwhelming.

Until now, though, it has only been the stage itself that has benefited from the ambience of the location, unique in Austria, whereas the path used by visitors to get from the parking lot to their seats in the auditorium and back always was an unatmospheric, merely functional accessway.

©Petra Schneidhofer

©Petra Schneidhofer

©Hertha Hurnaus

©Hertha Hurnaus

158

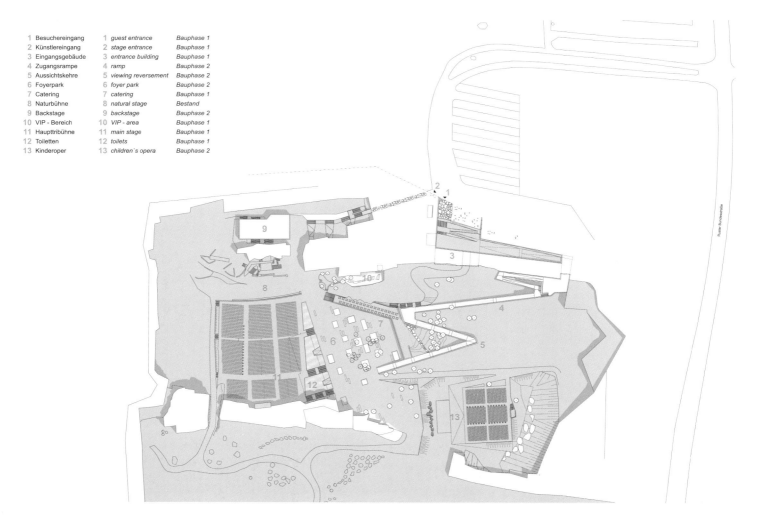

1	Besuchereingang	1	guest entrance	Bauphase 1
2	Künstlereingang	2	stage entrance	Bauphase 1
3	Eingangsgebäude	3	entrance building	Bauphase 1
4	Zugangsrampe	4	ramp	Bauphase 2
5	Aussichtskehre	5	viewing reversement	Bauphase 2
6	Foyerpark	6	foyer park	Bauphase 2
7	Catering	7	catering	Bauphase 1
8	Naturbühne	8	natural stage	Bestand
9	Backstage	9	backstage	Bauphase 2
10	VIP - Bereich	10	VIP - area	Bauphase 1
11	Haupttribüne	11	main stage	Bauphase 1
12	Toiletten	12	toilets	Bauphase 1
13	Kinderoper	13	children`s opera	Bauphase 2

©Hertha Hurnaus

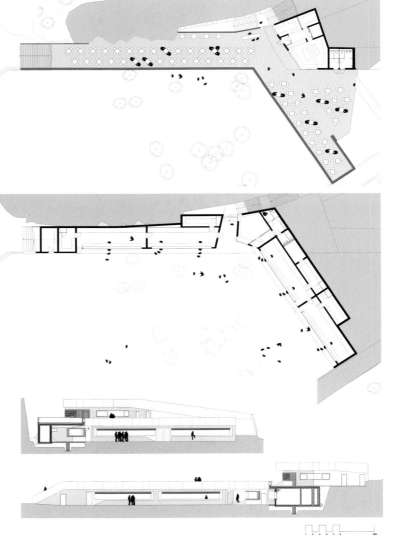

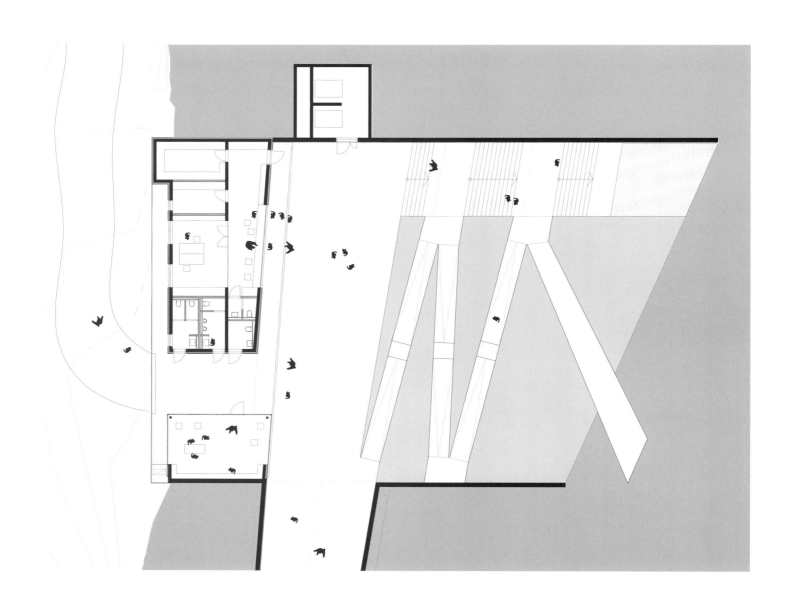

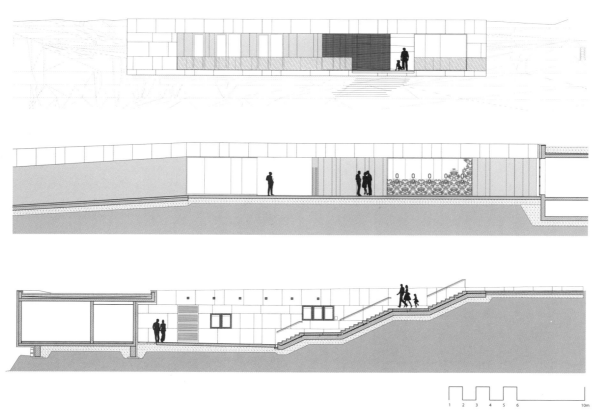

©Hertha Hurnaus

©Hertha Hurnaus

163

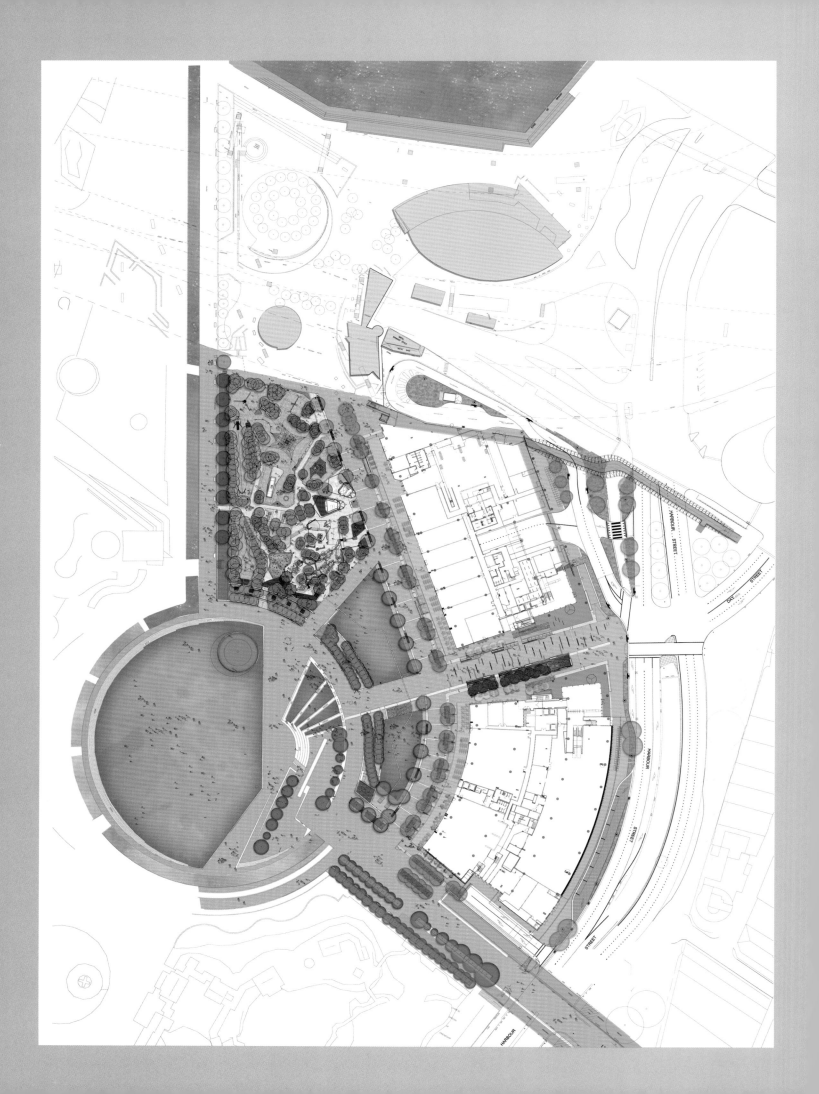

Design Agency: *ASPECT Studios*

Photography: *Florian Groehn*

Location: *Sydney, Australia*

Area: *15,000 m²*

Darling Quarter

General Description:

Darling Harbor South — or "Darling Quarter" as it is now known — is one of Australia's most visited destinations, and the redevelopment of its public domain has been a major place-making transformation project for Sydney. The 1.5 hectare project includes a retail terrace, public park, two six-star commercial buildings, a

new pedestrian street, and its centerpiece — at 4,000 m² — is the largest children's play space in the Sydney CBD. The unique water play area brings Darling Harbor's industrial heritage to the fore and establishes Darling Quarter as a regional destination.

Design Concept:

There are two keys to transform the Darling Quarter into a high quality family-centric precinct. The first key is that two bold pedestrian north-south and east-west links connect the precinct to Sydney city, Chinatown and Cockle Bay. Activated by cafes and retail activities, they become the framework for the public domain design. The second key has been to recognize that its public spaces must support family activities and allow social interaction between families and other users. And throughout Darling Quarter there is a strong focus on social and environmental sustainability.

Design Details:

Darling Quarter's unique play space creates an adventurous, innovative and highly interactive play experience. Its design recalls Darling Harbor's historic waterfront landscape setting by creating an intricately detailed abstracted river environment. Extensive research led to beautifully crafted water play elements being sourced from Germany and used in Australia for the first time. Sluice gates, hand pumps and an Archimedes screw allow children to direct water movement up and through channels back into a myriad of sculptural concrete streams folded in a highly sculpted landscape.

The water play area is complimented by a 'dry' playground space that features sand pits, a flying fox, giant climbing nets and huge family slides built for groups to use together. Amenities, a café, shade structures and stepped seating areas for parents.

Throughout the play spaces, interaction with nature and natural materials is fundamental. Artificial materials such as rubber surfaces are minimized. Play experiences include a wide array of physical sensations which are challenging, encourage development of agility and strength, and include an acceptable level of risk to engender a culture of children taking manageable risks through play.

In order to insist on social and environmental sustainability, rainwater is harvested in a 300,000 liter storage tank and distributed throughout the public domain for irrigation and water features. A new, energy efficient lighting strategy creates night-time ambience and activation. The post-top lights use best available technology, energy efficient lights, and a dimming system that reduces energy consumption by 60% compared to the current Darling Harbor precinct lights.

ASPECT Studios also designed two green roof terraces and community gardens as part of the precinct's new six-star rated Commonwealth Bank Australia building and for use by the 6,000 bank staff.

With its emphasis on premium quality materials and highly sustainable initiatives, Darling Quarter has set a new public space benchmark for Darling Harbor.

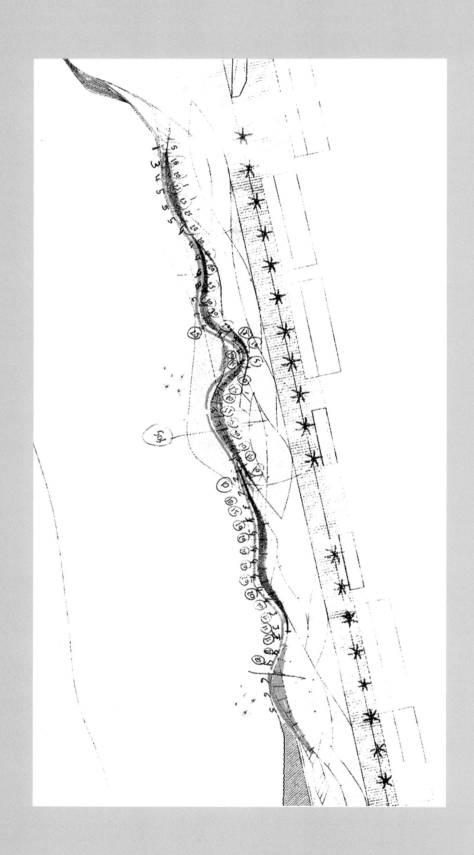

Design Agency: OAB

Designer: Xavier Martí Galí, Carlos Ferrater

Photography: Alejo Bagué

Location: Benidorm, Spain

Area: 18,000 m²

Seafront of Benidorm

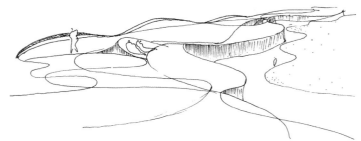

General Description:

Benidorm is perhaps the single most paradigmatic Spanish city of the massive industry of leisure and tourism, a city of an extremely high density concentrated in a tiny territory. The promenade in Benidorm, is a new transitional location between built city and the natural space of sea and beach.

Design Concept:

In the competition for the remodeling of the 1.5-kilometer-long West Beach Promenade, the architects proposed a radical innovation. Not only a borderline of protection, a hinge between town and sea, the construction will also be a public place that is conducive to many different activities.

Design Details:

The promenade, a place with a life of its own, has organic lines, a reminder of natural wave forms that generate an ensemble of honeycombed surfaces that juggle light and shadow, a series of convexities and concavities that gradually construct a set of platforms and levels that provide areas for play, meeting, leisure or contemplation. The surfaces of the promenade intersect, move off and change level, thus generating jutting platforms and concave and convex shapes without ever invading the area of sand.

A nexus of sinuous interwoven lines sets up the different spaces and adopts various natural and organic shapes evocative of the fractal structure of a cliff, as well as the motion of waves and tides.

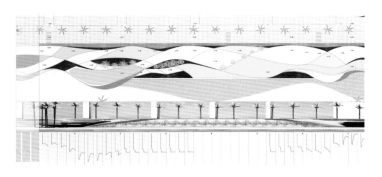
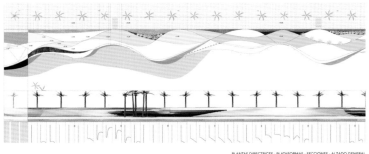

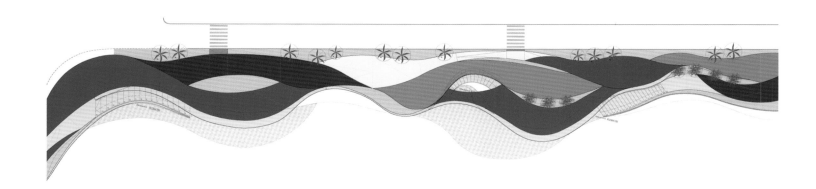

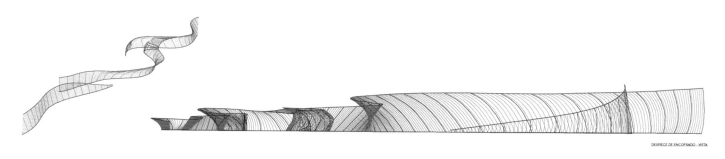

DESPIECE DE ENCOFRADO · VISTA

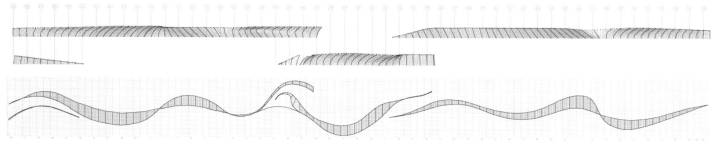

DESPIECE DE ENCOFRADO · PLANTA Y SECCIÓN

172

The promenade is structured in different layers: a first structural layer creates the perimeter line in white concrete; another textured layer with paving in different colors; and a last layer of street furniture and natural features like water and vegetation. All these contribute to a homogeneous location with its own personality; as well as being a predecessor to the new architecture of the 21st century by combining building technology and nature in a single whole.

Its layout will resolve the natural runoff of rainwater, allow for the support of collectors and infrastructure networks, eliminate architectonic barriers, link the beach with the underground car parks and thus become a complex strip of transition between the town and beach.

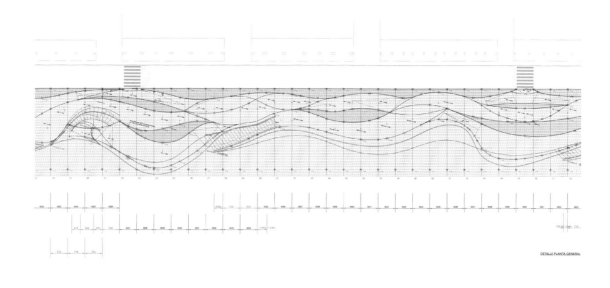

DETALLE PLANTA GENERAL

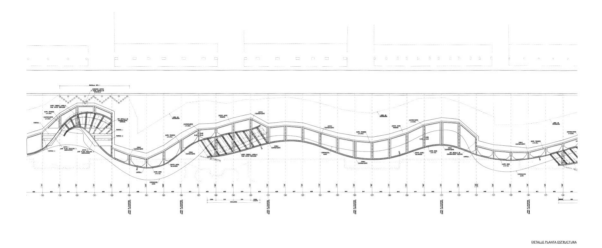

DETALLE PLANTA ESTRUCTURA

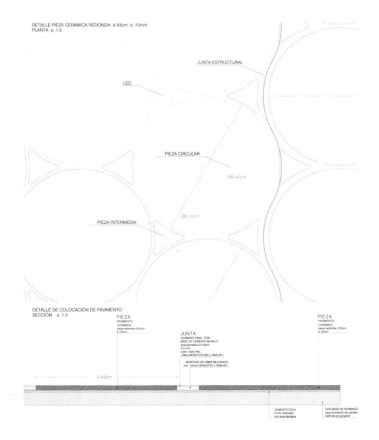

DETALLE PIEZA CERÁMICA REDONDA d:43cm e: 15mm
PLANTA e. 1:5

JUNTA ESTRUCTURAL

LED

PIEZA CIRCULAR

Ø0.43cm

PIEZA INTERMEDIA

Ø0.12cm

DETALLE DE COLOCACIÓN DE PAVIMENTO
SECCIÓN e. 1:5

PIEZA
PAVIMENTO-
CERÁMICA
pieza redonda d:25cm
e.15mm

JUNTA
ACABADO FINAL CON
BASE DE CEMENTO BLANCO
granulometría 0-0.3mm
e:3 mm
color: carta RAL
(SIKA MONOTON 620 o SIMILAR)

MORTERO DE OBRA MEJORADO
min. 10mm(SIKALATEX o SIMILAR)

PIEZA
PAVIMENTO-
CERÁMICA
pieza redonda d:25cm
e.15mm

0.43cm

CEMENTO COLA
6 mm colocado
con llana dentada

SUB-BASE DE HORMIGÓN
para formación de pendier
definida en proyecto

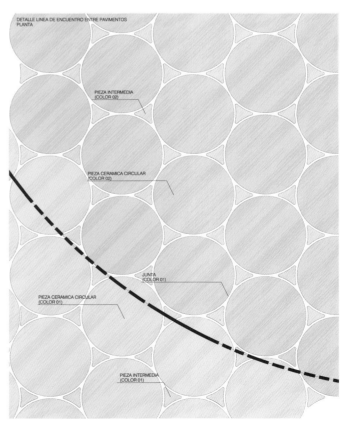

DETALLE LÍNEA DE ENCUENTRO ENTRE PAVIMENTOS
PLANTA

PIEZA INTERMEDIA
(COLOR 02)

PIEZA CERÁMICA CIRCULAR
(COLOR 02)

JUNTA
(COLOR 01)

PIEZA CERÁMICA CIRCULAR
(COLOR 01)

PIEZA INTERMEDIA
(COLOR 01)

DETALLE PAVIMENTO CERÁMICO

Design Agency: ASPECT Studios
Photography: Simon Wood
Location: Tweed Heads, Australia
Area: 49, 000 m²

Jack Evans Boat Harbor

General Description:

Jack Evans Boat Harbor is located at the mouth of the Tweed River, on the border of New South Wales and Queensland, and the new shoreline and aquatic recreation precinct were framed by 4.9 hectares of parkland. It reveals the singular beauty of the ever-shifting inter-tidal zone as an inhabitable landscape.

Design Concept:

Jack Evans Boat Harbor is intended to provide the impetus for the critical economic revitalization of Tweed Heads, and create a diverse, vibrant, culturally rich, recreational and tourism centerpiece for the town center.

Design Details:

The primary organizational element of the design is a simple, stepped, concrete gesture that frames the harbor edge. Its modular design provides a perfect platform for this landscape, and offers a refined solution to a complex hydrological environment subject to tidal, river and coastal climatic pressures.

A series of distinct relationships with the water develop along the harbor edge — a new beach and beach deck, a new rocky headland, an "urban pier", boardwalk, water amphitheatre, swimming areas, fishing points and opportunities for watercraft, all of them are designed to withstand frequent tidal and storm surge inundation, and to "future proof" the surrounding parklands against the effects of climate change and sea level rise.

Through its steps, ramps, rock sea walls, tidal pools, the water front design reveals the processes of time and tide at the transition between the Tweed River and the sea.

In addition, the reshaping of the shoreline has enabled the development of an "all abilities" access ramp to the water at all tidal levels, a unique recreational opportunity for the area.

The planting design has been developed in response to the variable salinity levels present on the intertidal shoreline zone, and wind exposure effects. The design retains many of the successful and significant tree specimens, and these help ground the new project into its context. The new revetment wall has been designed to facilitate the growth of mangroves.

Cultural gardens, an artwork "story wall" and space for public, community and performance art will showcase the regions rich local Aboriginal and European heritage. The project is the culmination of extensive indigenous and community consultation and creates a public space conducive to increased local and visitor recreational use, whilst protecting and promoting the natural beauty and environment of the area.

The parklands have become an informal "town square", a place for meeting, weekend markets, and with areas for memorials, children's play spaces and generous green banks for relaxation. Each park experience is connected by the active spine to the park and its constantly shifting revelation of the edge between land and water.

183

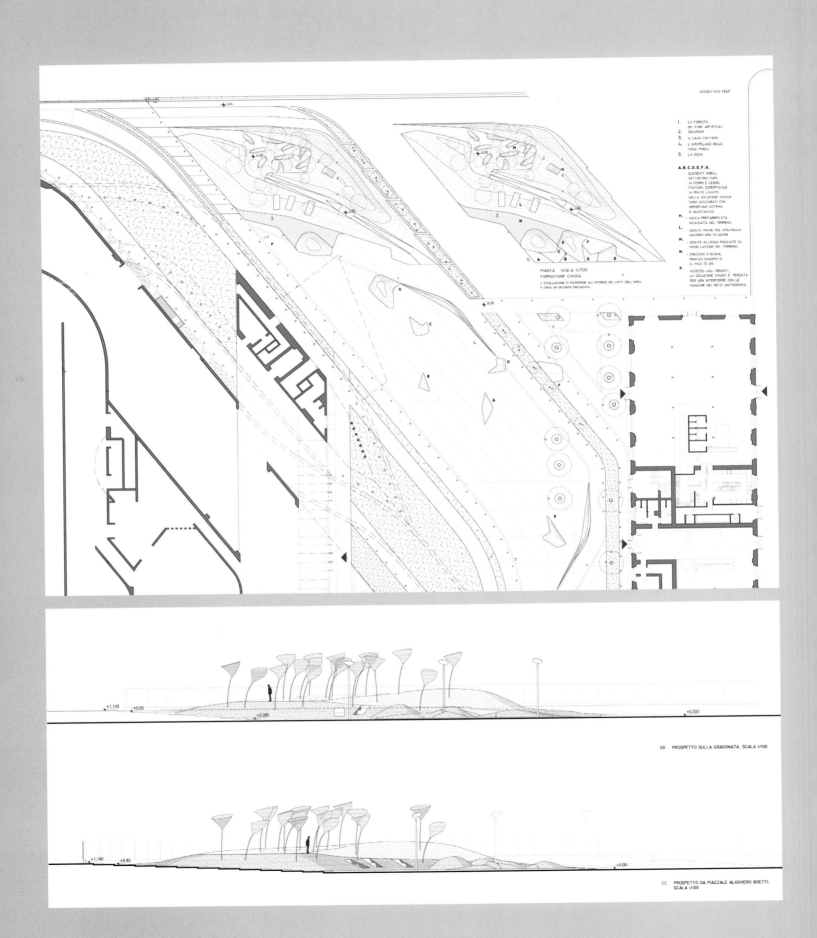

1. LA FORESTA
   DEI FIORI ARTIFICIALI
2. SOLARIUM
3. IL LAGO COSTIERO
4. L'ARCIPELAGO DELLE
   ISOLE MOBILI
5. LA DUNA

A.B.C.D.E.F.G.
ELEMENTI MOBILI,
SOTTOSTRUTTURA
IN FERRO E LEGNO.
FINITURA SUPERFICIALE
IN PRATO LAVATO.
NELLA SOLUZIONE CHIUSA
SONO ASSICURATI CON
OPPORTUNO SISTEMA
DI BLOCCAGGIO.

H. VASCA PREFABBRICATA
INCASSATA NEL TERRENO.

L. SEDUTE INCISE NEL DISLIVELLO,
SAGOMATURA IN LEGNO.

M. SEDUTE IN LEGNO POGGIATE SU
MODELLAZIONE DEL TERRENO.

N. SPECCHIO D'ACQUA,
PROFILO SAGOMATO
H. MAX 15 CM.

P. ACCESSO AGLI IDRANTI,
LA SOLUZIONE CHIUSA E' PENSATA
PER NON INTERFERIRE CON LE
MANOVRE DEI MEZZI ANTINCENDIO.

PIANTA SCALA 1/200
FORMAZIONE CHIUSA.
L'ISTALLAZIONE SI RICOMPONE ALL'INTERNO DEI LIMITI DELL'AREA
E CREA UN SECONDO PAESAGGIO.

BB PROSPETTO SULLA GRADONATA. SCALA 1/100

CC PROSPETTO DA PIAZZALE ALIGHIERO BOETTI.
SCALA 1/100

Design Agency: stARTT

Designer: S. Capra, C. Castaldo, F. Colangeli, A. Valentini

Light consultant and realization: Viabizzuno

Green technology consultant: M. Briziarelli

Photography: stARTT, Cesare Querci

Location: Rome, Italy

Area: 600 m²

184-189

Whatami

General Description:

Whatami, the corruption of "What am I", is based on the manufacturing of an artificial archipelago-hill, generating smaller green areas in the garden and potentially outside the museum. The hill works as a garden, injecting "green" into the concrete plateau of the museum's outdoor space, allowing it to serve as a stage and/or parterre for concerts and other events, or as a space to rest and look at the museum itself.

Design Concept:

The project manifests the artificial/natural relation as condition of metropolis culture.

Design Details:

The artificial landscape will be punctuated by large "flowers" providing light during the day, shadow in night time. It is a public cityscape used 24 hours changing its frequentation during the day: in the morning a refreshing summer place for families with children, in the afternoon set for museum's events, in the night lounge urban place for young generations.

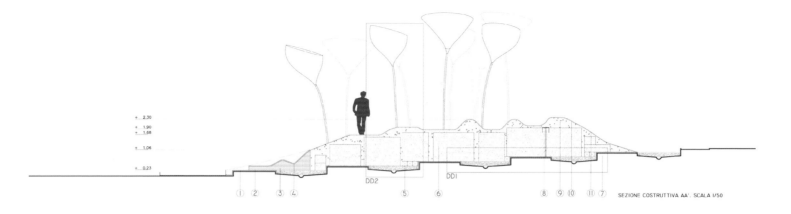

SEZIONE COSTRUTTIVA AA'. SCALA 1/50

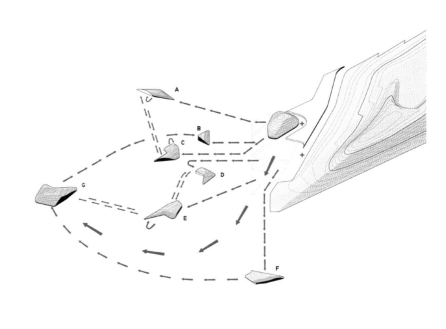

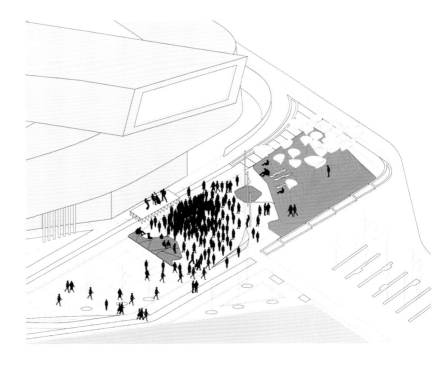

©Cesare Querci

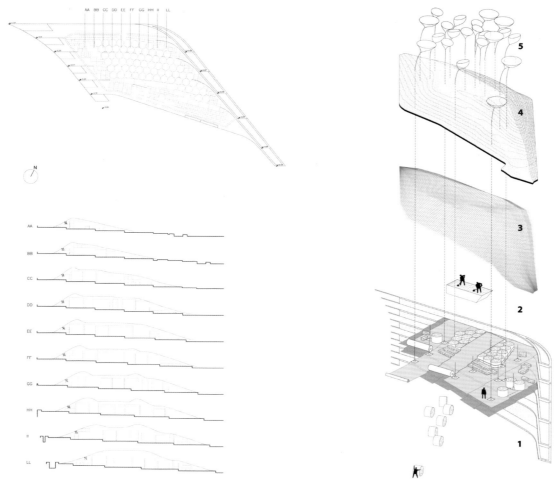

Design Agency: AllesWirdGut Architektur

Creative Director: AllesWirdGut

Photography: Roger Wagner

Location: Esch-sur-Alzette, Luxembourg

Area: 10, 000 m²

City Square Developing

General Description:

City Square Developing (LUX), a city development project was constructed in Luxembourg on the ground of a former steel mill.

Design Concept:

The disused industrial site's atmosphere was characterized by wideness and roughness as well as pioneer plants such as mosses and birch. The former situation is necessarily literally covered by the new use and new design. The architects' major goal was to let the now hidden qualities shine through the redesign.

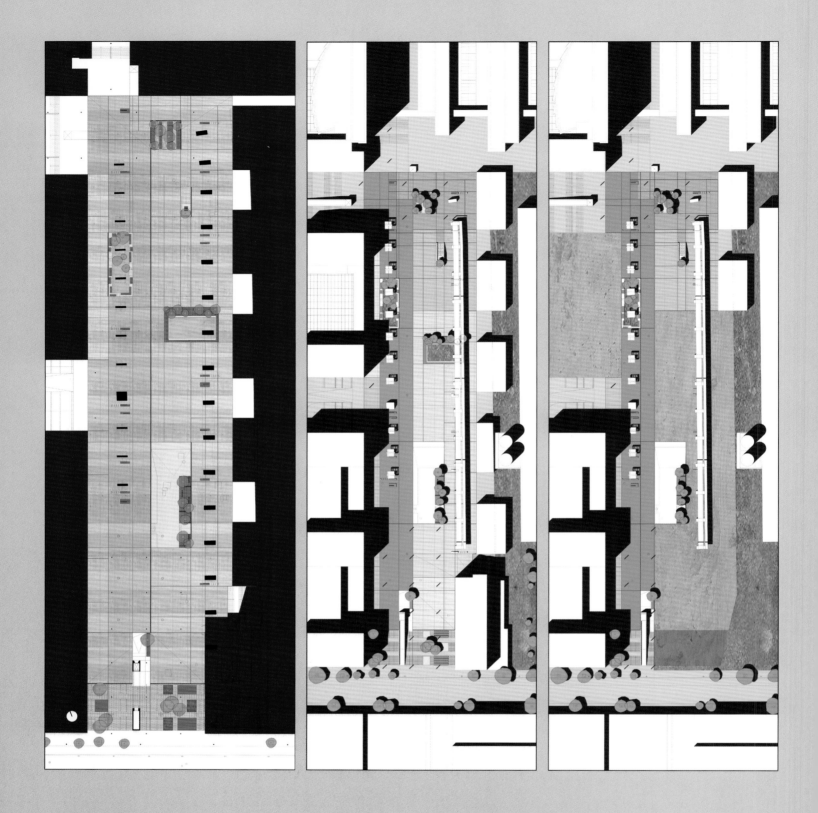

Design Details:

Seating areas and new trees are concentrated into islands, which leave empty large areas of space and also serve as focal points in this emptiness.

Aging-capable materials such as concrete, wood and untreated steel in combination with rough detailing make it possible for the patina of the past to return.

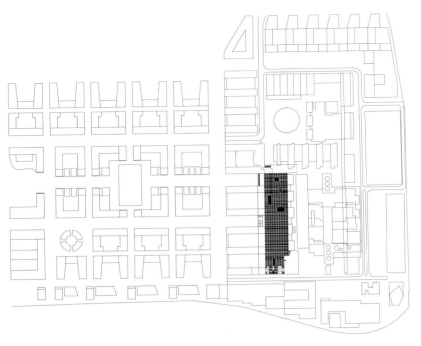

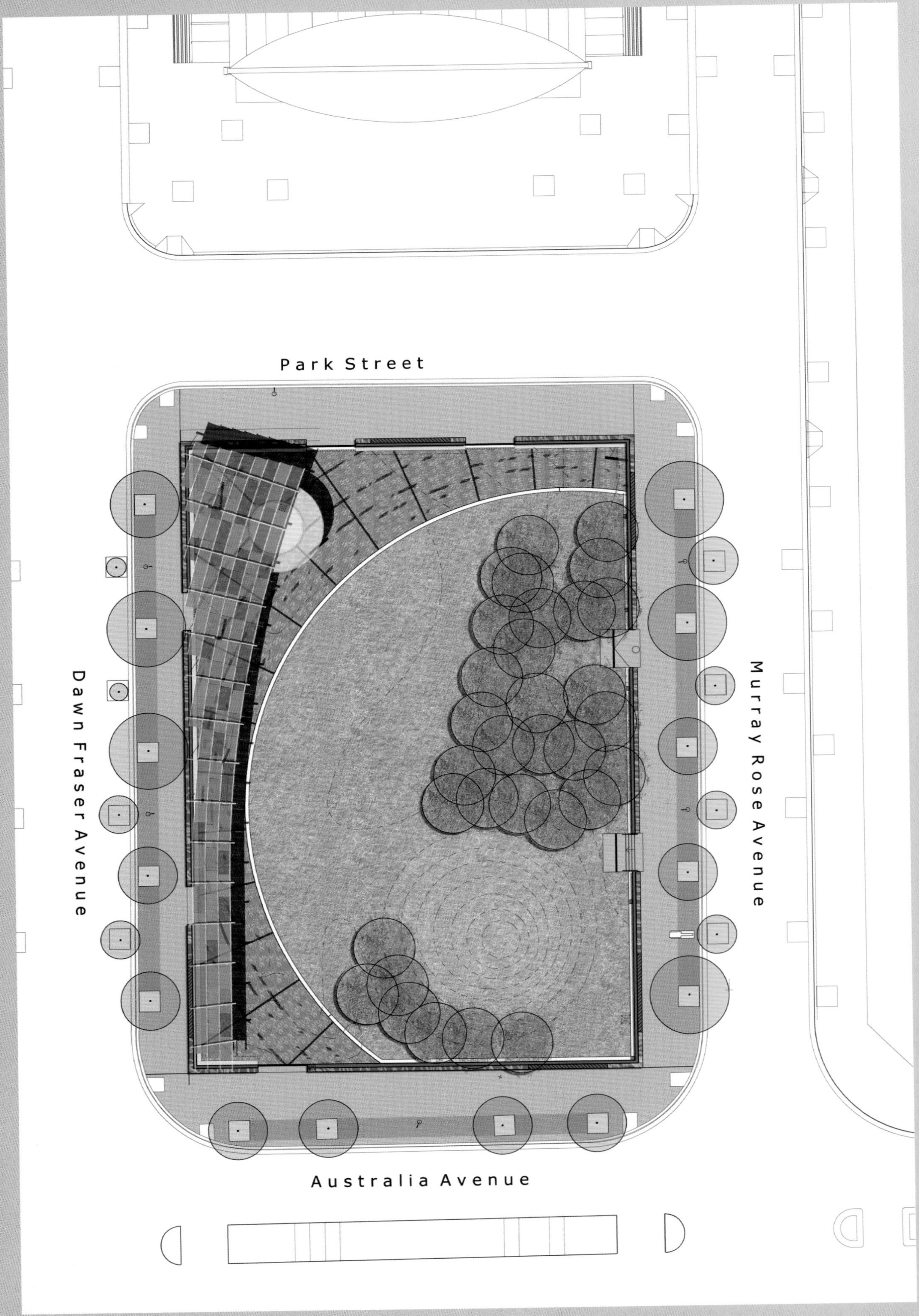

Park Street

Dawn Fraser Avenue

Murray Rose Avenue

Australia Avenue

Design Agency: ASPECT Studios
Photography: Simon Wood, Sacha Coles
Location: Sydney, Australia
Area: 4, 000 m²

Jacaranda Square "The Everyday Stadium"

General Description:

Jacaranda Square "The Everyday Stadium" is the first in a series of new public spaces of the new residential and business community of Sydney Olympic Park — site of the Sydney Olympic Games of 2000. The highly strategic design creates a vibrant, active and sustainable town center, interfacing a new town center with adjacent massed sporting facilities and large event spaces.

Design Concept:

Jacaranda Square is an urban park for passive recreation and community gathering. The name "The Everyday Stadium" is both a gentle, ironic nod to the Olympic legacy and the surrounding context of the site, as well as a description of the design concept. It is also a meaningful, memorable and sustainable public space, central to the development of the larger Sydney Olympic Park community.

Design Details:

The stadium form here finds expression through three main elements: a defined built and tiered edge, a useable green center, and shade providing canopies.

The edge is defined by a wall conceived as a brick skin to the outside face of the square, and a shifting precast concrete section to the interior of the square. The wall is a seat, a lounge and a protective and edge defining element. The angled outside surface provides places to lean, while inside an informal rhythm of concrete elements allows users to relax.

The wall both separates the square from its surrounds — declaring a change of scale and space — and through its materiality celebrates the industrial history of the area. The wall's green glazed pixelation of bricks "prixelation" manages to shift the built form towards hedge rather than seat or wall.

Inside the square, the recycled brick edge to the grassed center plays off against the sheen on the wall's glazed bricks, and the circular patterning emphasizes the geometries at work throughout the design and its adjacencies. Materiality has been used to express place. A grassed, ovoid mound is the centerpiece of the square, and the primary space for informal gathering rest, relaxation and play.

"The Everyday Stadium" canopy is both built and natural, and provides long perimeters of shade. The built canopy is a unifying element paralleling the active side of the space. The pattern and play of its colored mesh panels are an element that can be viewed from above and in the round, and operate as a functional device for providing weather protection and for harvesting rainwater. The natural canopy is a grove of lemon scented gums, Corymbia citriodora, which fan across the site, providing long term shade, a much needed element in the hot summer months.

The final result is colorful, clean and green: a series of modular precast-concrete lounge suites, a canopy of polychrome greens, and walls of glazed pixilated bricks set amongst a treed urban landscape.

ELIZABETH MACARTHUR BAY

ELIZABETH MACARTHUR BAY

ELIZABETH MACARTHUR BAY

LINE OF SEAWALL UNDER - LOCATION TO BE CONFIRMED

LINE OF SEAWALL UNDER

LINE OF SEAWALL UNDER

PYRMONT
POINT PARK

PIRRAMA ROAD

PIRRAMA ROAD

PIRRAMA ROAD

HERBERT STREET

HERBERT STREET

PLAYGROUND

HARRIS STREET

Design Agency: *ASPECT Studios*
Photography: *Florian Groehn, Adrian Boddy*
Location: *Sydney, Australia*
Area: *18, 000 m²*

Pirrama Park

General Description:

The 1.8 hectares of waterfront that is Pirrama Park began with community action which successfully prevented the State Government's sale of this public land to residential developers. When the City of Sydney Council purchased the former Water Police site, what was a previously alienated and fenced-off post-industrial concrete slab became in time a richly varied urban waterfront parkland for the people of Sydney.

Design Concept:

The park design interprets the site's successive shorelines and rich maritime associations. The name, Pirrama, is taken from the original Aboriginal name for Pyrmont Peninsula. The location of the original shoreline informs the placement of the generous promenade. The expression of its landside elements is influenced by natural terrain, and the geometry and form of its waterside elements respond more directly to the reclaimed post-industrial condition. Through its exposed encampments and harbor reclamation, the site tells a part of Sydney's wharf making history.

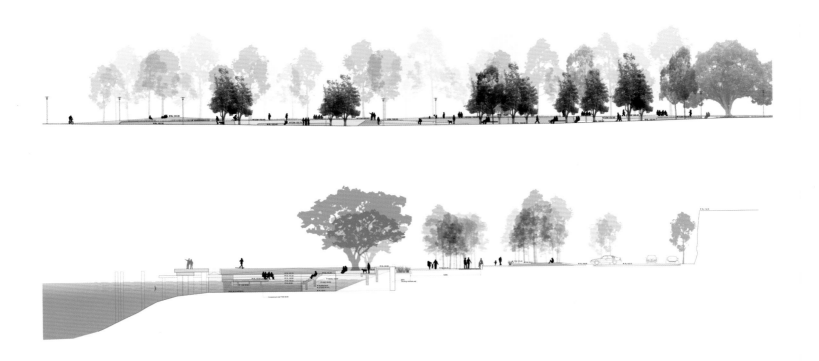

Design Details:

Pirrama Park presented a flat, featureless base — a legacy of its industrial past. The designers inherited a slab of concrete with barely 2 meters of variation across the site.

The robust wharf apron and a central long, low retaining wall underpin the geometry of the park. Supplementary wharf structures have been removed to reinstate and build on an earlier and historic relationship of Harris Street to Sydney Harbor. A wide terrace corresponding to the Harris Street alignment now extends over the harbor edge, its underside lapped by high water spring tides.

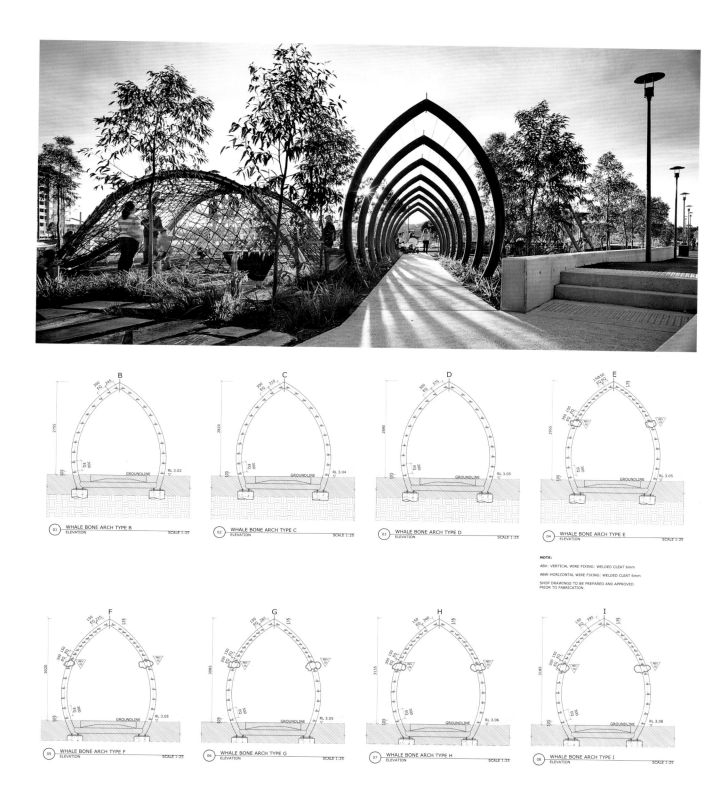

"The Point and Green" and "The Sheltered Bay" occupy platforms previously reclaimed from Sydney Harbor. The stepped platforms north and south of the bay occupy the inter-tidal zone and intensify the experience of twice daily rhythms of capturing, flooding and retreating water. They have become social places for landing small watercraft, wading and swimming, fishing and yarning.

The integrated site specific play space is an attraction for both locals and district visitors alike. The water play elements, reclaimed sandstone and natural setting allude to the once famed beach and "Pyrmont Spring".

The waterfront "Community Square" is a sunny, sheltered place that can accommodate a range of public uses including cultural events and performances, meetings, markets, festivals and the like, appropriate to the evolving urbanity of Pyrmont Point.

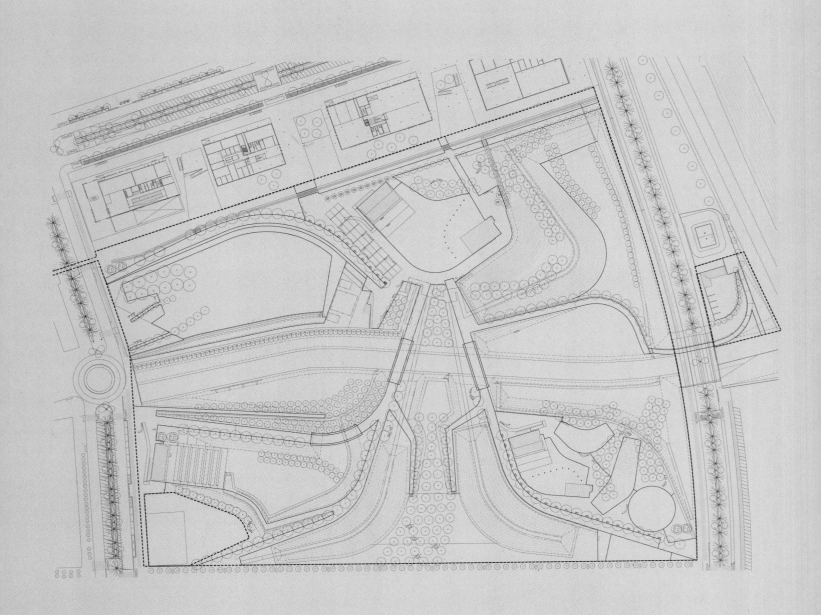

Design Agency: BATLLE I ROIG ARCHITECTS

Designer: Enric Batlle, Joan Roig

Photography: Jordi Surroca

Location: Barcelona, Spain

Area: 100, 000 m²

Marina Park in Viladecans, Barcelona

General Description:

The expansion of Viladecans, as the vast majority of towns located on the left riverbank of the River Llobregat, has not only been hampered due to the riverbeds (rieras), but also has ignored them until they became outdoor sewers where waste waters were discharged and demolition debris was accumulated.

Design Concept:

The recovery project for the Riera de Sant Climent aimed to consider the riverbed as a natural corridor that would work as a link between the agricultural park and the mountain across the town. This could turn the "riera" into an urban park, recovering its native vegetation and turning the covered sections into wooded promenades.

Design Details:

Marina Park emerges as the culmination of the Riera de Sant Climent's green corridor. The riverbed is still uncovered along the park, thus creating some lateral impoundments that, in case of floods or overflowing of the river, they would act as temporary accumulation and lamination pools for rainwater. The groves and pathways system that comes from the north opens up and runs freely through the park, organizing diversified itineraries. These pathways are sorted into two types: those that are located at the field level and those that, by means of modifications of the topography or of the construction of walkways, run through higher elevations and allow pedestrians to cross the riverbed or the surrounding streets. These topographic dunes enable the generation of different areas where we can locate the uses of the park: the natural amphitheater, the fairground, the children's playground, the "Oloretum" (aromatic plants), the pinewoods and the picnic areas.

The park also aims to create a sustainable hydraulic system for the collection and infiltration of rainwater, as well as for the concept and irrigation system. The collection of rainwater is carried out by a system of vegetal canals of large section that, even being traced with very soft inclination, they can conduct the water to the designated inundation areas, thus avoiding sending it to the general sewerage system. This arrangement aims to maximize the infiltration of rainwater to the subsoil and its utilization as natural irrigation.

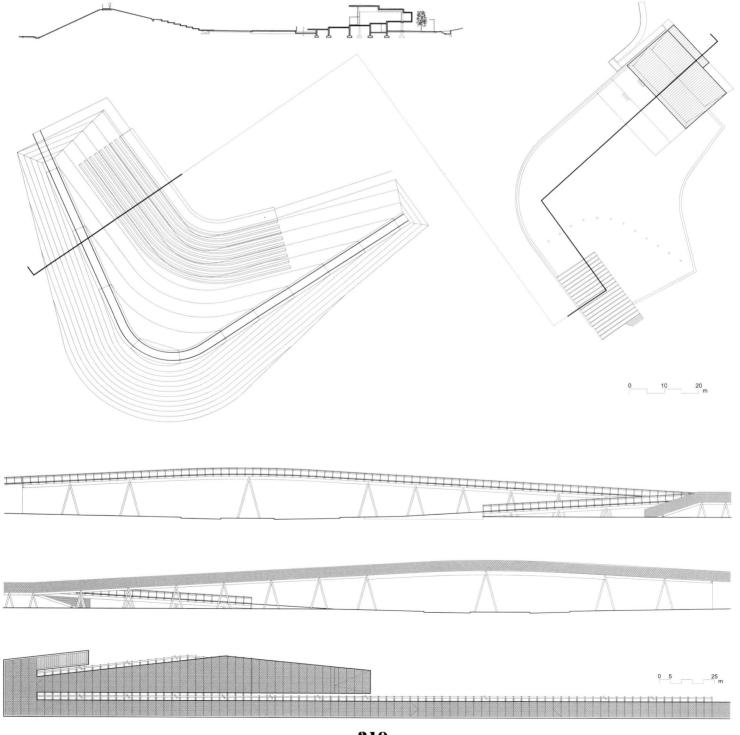

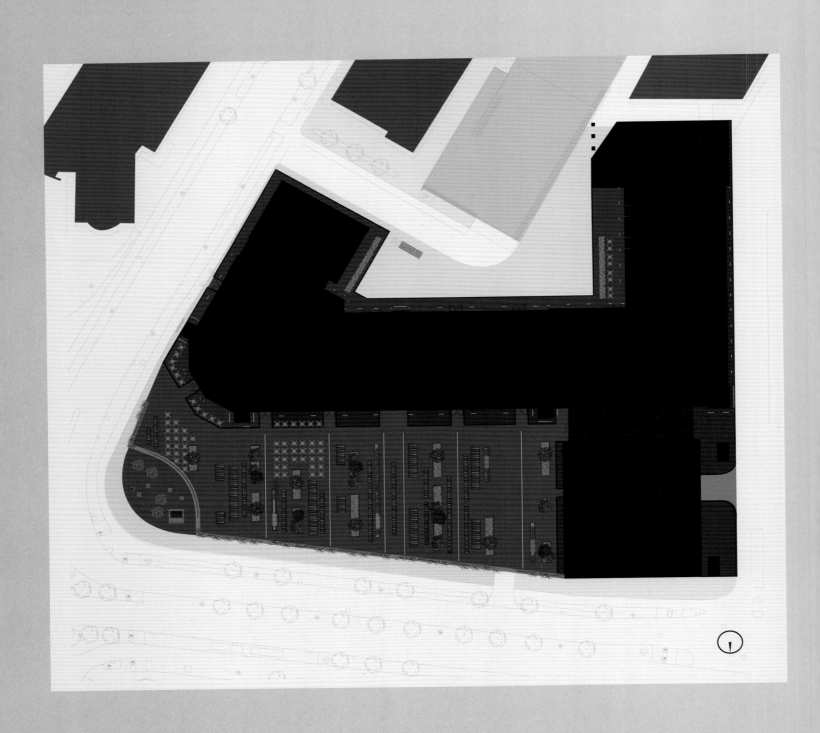

Design Agency: *Buro Lubbers*
Designer: *Buro Lubbers*
Photography: *Buro Lubbers*
Location: *Eindhoven, the Netherlands*
Area: *5, 500 m²*

Mathilde Square

Concept

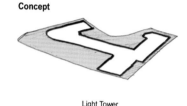

Light Tower

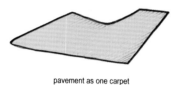

pavement as one carpet

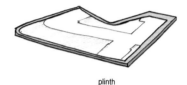

plinth

green oasis

General Description:

Mathilde Square was a challenge not only in terms of its design and urban integration requirements, but also in its demand for technical finesse. To escape the frenetic activity of downtown Eindhoven, one can now relax in the green oasis at Mathilde Square. After shopping or a long day at the office, here one can quietly enjoy a drink on the terrace or sit down on a bench among lush plants.

Design Concept:

The amorphous form of the planning area demanded an exacting structure. The design concept is therefore based on rigid lines that run counter to the building. The unity of the design is accomplished by using consistent shapes and materials.

Design Details:

The surface is paved with just one material: a dark gray concrete slab resembling natural stone. This gray carpet is laid in a rigid, complex

pattern and is surrounded by a plinth that distinguishes the square from the building and also highlights the difference in level between the parking deck and the environment. The square becomes an enclave with its own distinctive identity. The difference in level distinguishes the hectic city life and the intimate and green area of the square. These divergent worlds are also emphasized by the fence around the square, which serves mainly as a security measure. Wisteria and roses overgrow the adjacent pergola and create a transparent

barrier, offering passersby a glimpse of the green atmosphere and the terraces.

Elongated Corten planters create a stripe pattern, producing alternating open and closed spaces that are suitable for routing and terraces. At several spaces between the container, the wooden benches and bicycle stands that vary in length, width and height are positioned. The robust color of the Corten steel, the warm look of natural wood and the gray pavement, form an interesting contrast to the white, gray and black tones of the building.

VIEW FENCING MATHILDESQUARE

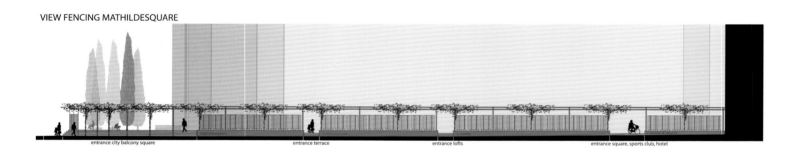

entrance city balcony square   entrance terrace   entrance lofts   entrance square, sports club, hotel

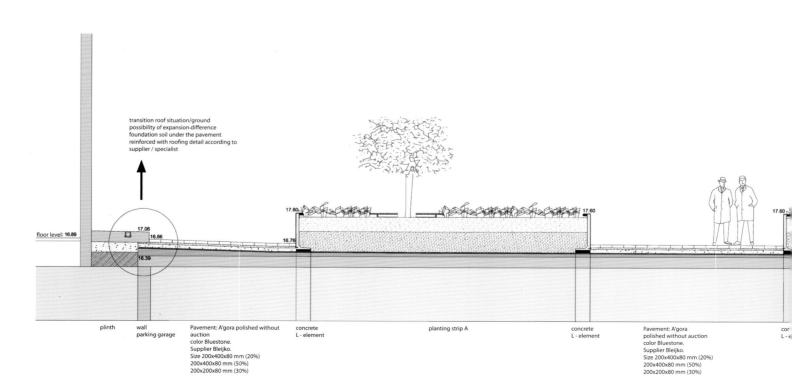

transition roof situation/ground
possibility of expansion difference
foundation soil under the pavement
reinforced with roofing detail according to
supplier / specialist

floor level: 16.89

17.06
16.86
16.39
16.76
16.39

17.60
17.60
17.60

| plinth | wall parking garage | Pavement: A'gora polished without auction color Bluestone. Supplier Bleijko. Size 200x400x80 mm (20%) 200x400x80 mm (50%) 200x200x80 mm (30%) | concrete L - element | planting strip A | concrete L - element | Pavement: A'gora polished without auction color Bluestone. Supplier Bleijko. Size 200x400x80 mm (20%) 200x400x80 mm (50%) 200x200x80 mm (30%) | cor L - |

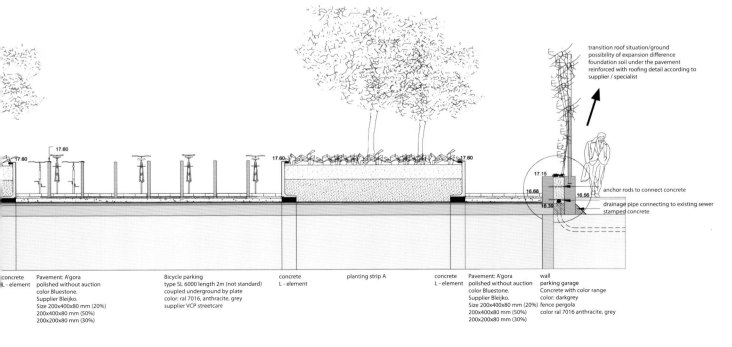

concrete
L - element

Pavement: A'gora
polished without auction
color Bluestone.
Supplier Bleijko.
Size 200x400x80 mm (20%)
200x400x80 mm (50%)
200x200x80 mm (30%)

Bicycle parking
type SL 6000 length 2m (not standard)
coupled underground by plate
color: ral 7016, anthracite, grey
supplier VCP streetcare

concrete
L - element

planting strip A

concrete
L - element

Pavement: A'gora
polished without auction
color Bluestone.
Supplier Bleijko.
Size 200x400x80 mm (20%)
200x400x80 mm (50%)
200x200x80 mm (30%)

wall
parking garage
Concrete with color range
color: darkgrey
fence pergola
color ral 7016 anthracite, grey

transition roof situation/ground
possibility of expansion difference
foundation soil under the pavement
reinforced with roofing detail according to
supplier / specialist

anchor rods to connect concrete

drainage pipe connecting to existing sewer
stamped concrete

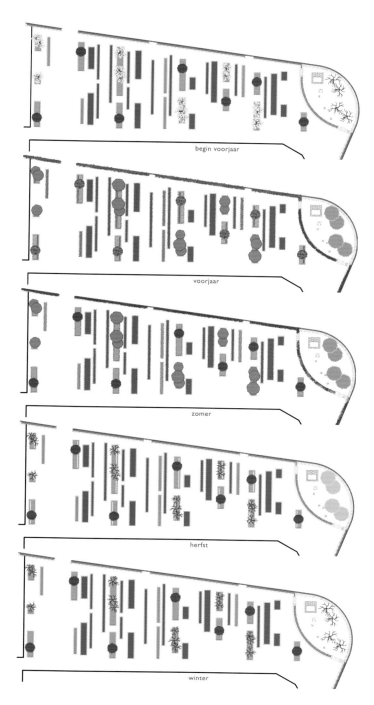

begin voorjaar

voorjaar

zomer

herfst

winter

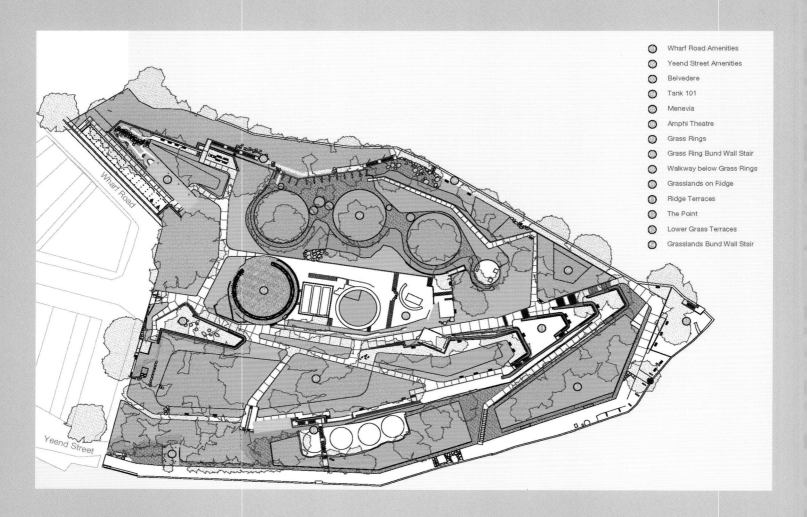

Wharf Road

Yeend Street

○ Wharf Road Amenities
○ Yeend Street Amenities
○ Belvedere
○ Tank 101
○ Menevia
○ Amphi Theatre
○ Grass Rings
○ Grass Ring Bund Wall Stair
○ Walkway below Grass Rings
○ Grasslands on Ridge
○ Ridge Terraces
○ The Point
○ Lower Grass Terraces
○ Grasslands Bund Wall Stair

Design Agency: McGregor Coxall

Designer: Philip Coxall, Adrian McGregor, Christian Borchert, Jeremy Gill, Kristin Spradbrow

Photography: Christian Borchert

Location: Sydney, Australia

Area: 25,000 m²

Ballast Point Park

General Description:

This multi award winning 2.5 ha post-industrial waterfront park is located on a contaminated former lubricant production site on the Birchgrove Peninsula in the inner reaches of Sydney harbor.

Design Concept:

The design embraces world leading sustainability principles to minimize the project's carbon footprint and ecologically rehabilitate the site. It reconciles the layers of history with forward looking new technologies to create a regionally significant urban park and combines readings of cultural heritage with environmental innovation to restore a green headland park for the local community.

Design Details:

The design challenges the architects' perception of materials and their use. Dominant new terrace walls sit atop the sandstone cliffs but these walls are not made of precious sandstone excavated from another site, rather from the rubble of our past. What once was called rubbish is now called beautiful. It is the new ballast. But it is more than this at play. It is the total composition of these recycled rubber filled cages, off set with concrete coping panels topped with fine grain railing, that allow these walls to sit confidently at the portal to the inner harbor.

Eight vertical axis wind turbines and an extract from a Les Murray poem, carved into recycled tank panels, forms a sculptural re-interpretation of the site's former largest storage tank. The wind turbines symbolize the future, a step away from our fossil fuelled past towards more sustainable renewable energy forms.

Its design strategy explores many innovative uses of construction techniques and materials, these range from re-enforced earth walls clad with recycled rubble in baskets, green star rated concrete using recycled materials in lieu of traditional components, recycled timbers for the buildings and park furniture as well as recycled soils, mulches and gravels. The planting for the site is provenance stock drawn from local plant communities that promotes the local gene pool as well as assist in the re-establishment of the local fauna.

The environmental approach is underpinned by use of provenance planting, storm water biofiltration, recycled materials, and wind turbines for renewable energy.

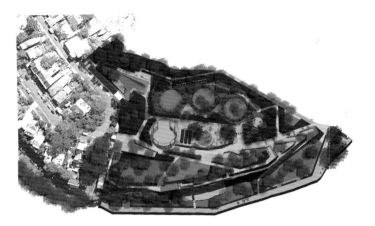

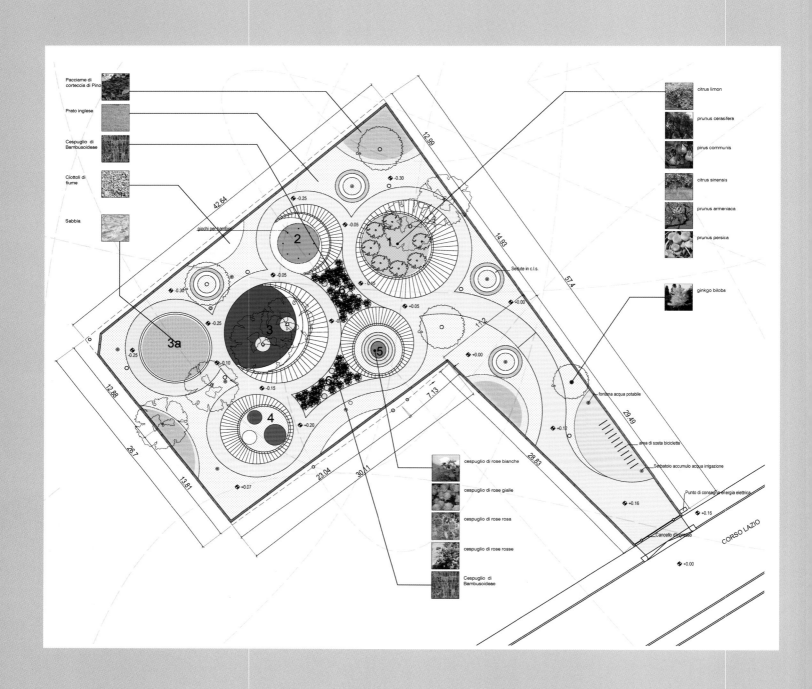

Pacciame di corteccia di Pino

Prato inglese

Cespuglio di Bambusoideae

Ciottoli di fiume

Sabbia

citrus limon

prunus cerasifera

pirus communis

citrus sinensis

prunus armeniaca

prunus persica

ginkgo biloba

giochi per bambini

Sedute in c.l.s.

fontana acqua potabile

area di sosta biciclette

Serbatoio accumulo acqua irrigazione

Punto di consegna energia elettrica

Cancello d'ingresso

CORSO LAZIO

cespuglio di rose bianche

cespuglio di rose gialle

cespuglio di rose rosa

cespuglio di rose rosse

Cespuglio di Bambusoideae

12.99

42.64

14.93

57.4

12.88

26.7

13.81

23.04

30.1

7.13

28.83

29.49

1
2
3
3a
4
5

-0.30
-0.25
-0.05
-0.05
-0.05
+0.05
+0.00
-0.30
-0.25
-0.10
-0.15
-0.25
-0.25
+0.00
+0.00
+0.07
+0.20
+0.12
+0.16
+0.16
+0.00

Design Agency: NABITO ARCHITECTS & PARTNERS	Location: Frosinone, Italy
Designer: Alessandra Faticanti, Roberto Ferlito, Luca Faticanti, Damiano Bauco, Gianluca Sanità	Area: 2, 000 m²
Photography: Claudia Pescatori	

Sensational Garden

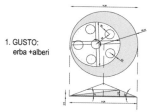
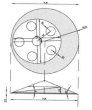

1. GUSTO:
erba +alberi

2.UDITO:
ciottoli

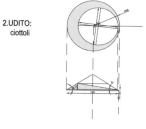

3.TATTO/piazza:
greenfloor

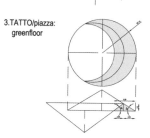

4.: OLFATTO
essenze
profumate

5. VISTA
rosaceae

General Description:

Sensational Garden represents the starting point of a big master-plan to renew and integrate the public spaces and the services to the housing neighborhood.

Design Concept:

Sensational Garden amplifies the idea of a relational space filling the social void with an explosive, playful, sensorial and interactive intimate room, like a personal living room in a public realm. Here users and citizens could find the joy of live, love and know each other again and make themselves comfortable with the entire neighborhood renewing the social sustainability of this site of the city.

Design Details:

The goal of the project is to invite users to a path in which scene are always changing. The user will have the sensation to discover always different spaces but with the same kind of characteristics.

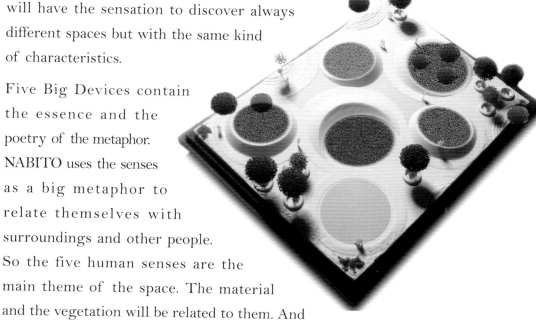

Five Big Devices contain the essence and the poetry of the metaphor. NABITO uses the senses as a big metaphor to relate themselves with surroundings and other people. So the five human senses are the main theme of the space. The material and the vegetation will be related to them. And

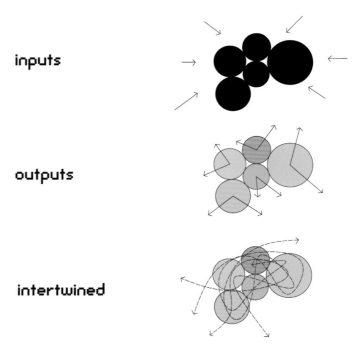

inputs

outputs

intertwined

to them. And a path, as the link between them, was designed to leave the spaces be revealed to a visitor little by little, so to induce and encourage the user to continue the experience. The smell is attracted by the support of the essences, the hearing from the game sound amplification, the view from the beautiful rose garden that you can feel the materials of the central cone, and the taste is stimulated by fruit trees in the largest support. The balanced blend of natural essences (trees, shrubs and flowers) and the artificial elements (cement and resin) make the garden easy to maintain durable and mutable during the time.

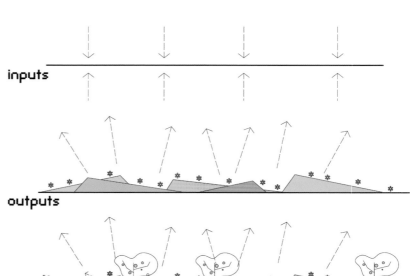

inputs

outputs

intertwined

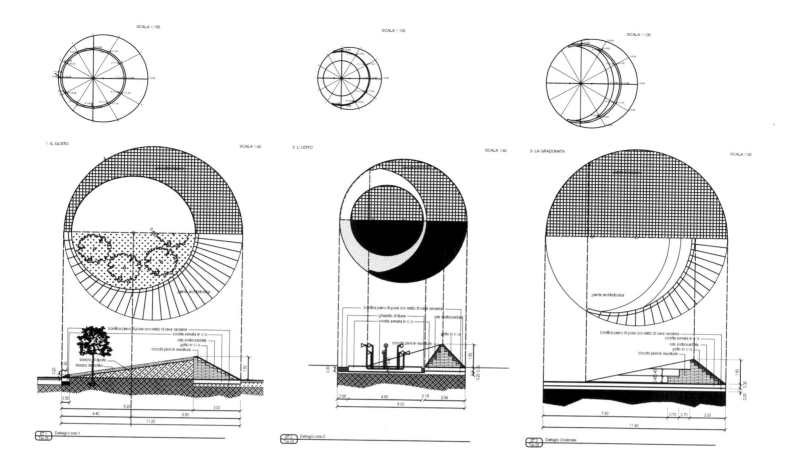

1. IL GUSTO   SCALA 1:50

2. L'UDITO   SCALA 1:50

3. LA GRADONATA   SCALA 1:50

pianta architettonica

bonifica piano di posa con misto di cava calcarea
soletta armata in c.l.s
rete elettrosaldata
getto in c.l.s
blocchi pieni in muratura
terreno di riporto
terreno da coltivo

0.20   0.30

0.50   8.20   3.00
4.40   6.80
11.20

DT 1   Dettaglio cono 1

pianta architettonica

bonifica piano di posa con misto di cava calcarea
ghiaietto di fiume
soletta armata in c.l.s
rete elettrosaldata
getto in c.l.s
blocchi pieni in muratura

0.30   0.20 0.30   1.50

0.68   4.60   0.18   2.54
8.00

DT 2   Dettaglio cono 2

pianta architettonica

bonifica piano di posa con misto di cava calcarea
soletta armata in c.l.s
rete elettrosaldata
getto in c.l.s
blocchi pieni in muratura

1.60   0.30 0.20

7.80   0.70 0.70   2.20
11.40

DT 3   Dettaglio Gradonata

Design Agency: *CREUSeCARRASCO*

Designer: *Juan Creus, Covadonga Carrasco*

Photography: *Xóan Piñón, CREUSeCARRASCO*

Location: *A Coruña, Spain*

Area: *13, 710 m²*

Harbor Remodelling Malpica

General Description:

This harbor redevelopment project, developed in conjunction with the Port Authority, is primarily focused on zones where public space can be created.

Design Concept:

The project emphasizes the potential for the improvement of a recurring situation in many Galician fishing village whose size prevents a "new slate" response: the fact that treatment of the few repeated elements, i.e., these organizational patterns, often hidden and with a neglected, intrinsically unattractive presence, can generate a different, perhaps unstructured, cubist type of beauty which is nevertheless a reflection of a direct, popular intentionality.

Design Details:

The harbor was analyzed as a place for interrelations and shelter, with the appeal of its fishing industry and its views; a unique location that makes its presence felt in the town with ramps, stairs and balconies.

The linear nature of the horseshoe-shaped harbor is exploited to the utmost with a promenade, accessible at an intermediate level that runs along the cliff, resting on outcrops and wall tops which inhabit it in a sense. The zone for rock climbers, gull's nests and ensconced rocks appear out of nowhere for strolling visitors. The intermediate layer, a chameleon camouflage, overlooks the harbor activity without interfering in it. Almost nobody remembers, but the pier deck has been set at the same grade level as the sluice, 6.10, which has improved the visual and spatial integration of the eastern side, while the wastewater duct which used to be in full view along the full length of the waterfront has been buried beneath a meter of backfill. The recovered wall base for house, many of them in stone, facilitates an interpretation of the cliff and its image.

One of the components of the town's memory, Murallón lookout, is expanded and separated from vehicular traffic. Buildings on the south descent from the harbor, including a warehouse, a workshop and the Red Cross building, are demolished to release and extend more space in a curve and propose, in continuity from this point, a new promenade to Punta da Plancha set on the stone wall at a constant 4.5 meters above the harbor platform. A Pancha is turned into a lookout and a ramp link to the ground. Along the way, the cliffs are treated with shotcrete and artificial gardens are planted. The workshop, which was initially to be moved to beneath the promenade, has finally been relocated as a unit inside an existing pavilion.

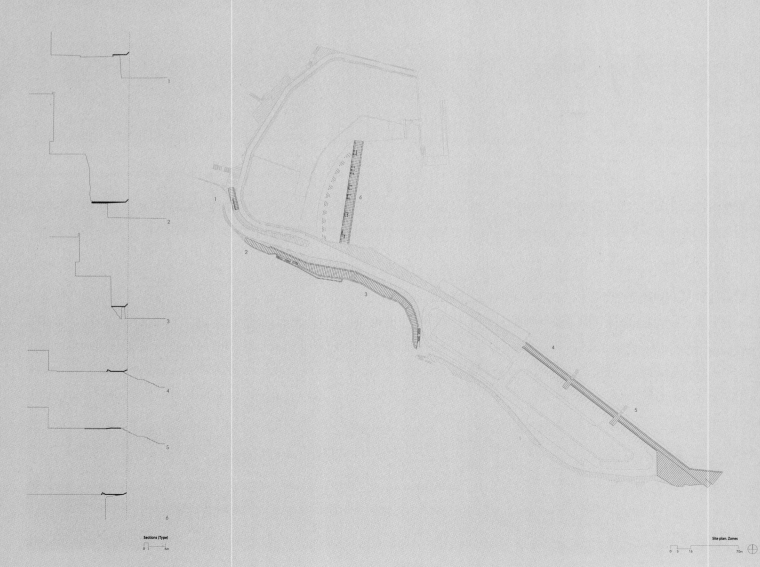

Sections (Type)

0 1   5m

Site plan. Zones

0 3   15   70m

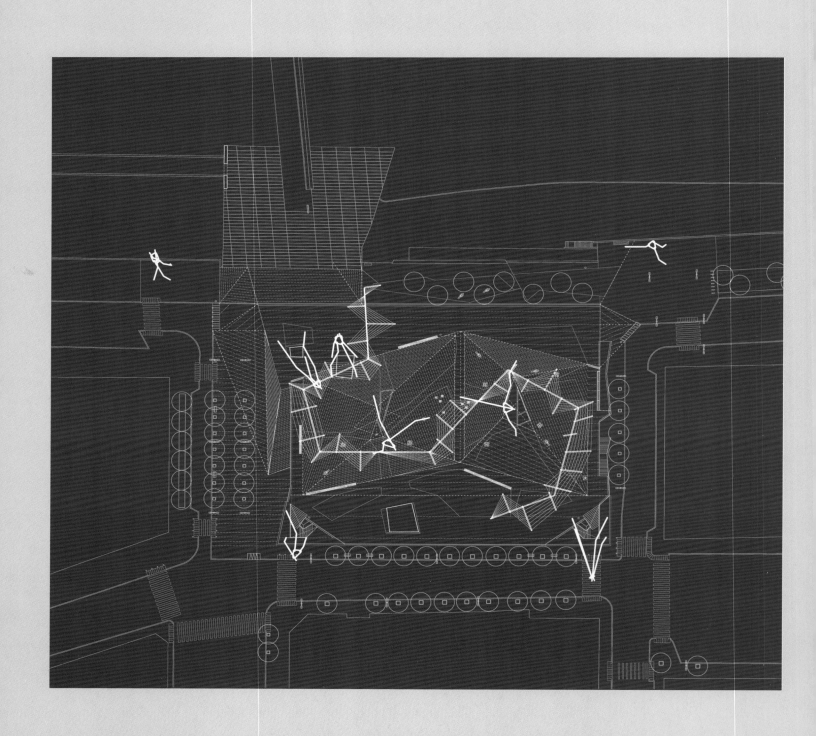

Design Agency: *mamen domingo ¡! ernest ferré architects*

Designer: *Mamen Domingo, Ernest Ferré*

Photography: *Jordi Bernadó*

Location: *Lleida, Spain*

Area: *8, 403 m²*

Blas Infante Square

General Description:

Blas Infante Square, a neighborhood place has been created by making use of the immediate environment. It's a place of rest, leisure, and neighborhood relationship, with shade and benches, playground, grass and floral vegetation following the route of the pergola as protection for the summer.

Design Concept:

The proposal represents and symbolizes the new centrality that Blas Infante Square offers in a contemporary way. The project is developed from the duality of the two scales that are mixed: the scale of the neighborhood, immediate environment, and a larger size, the city and its historic center.

Design Details:

The existence of a newly built underground parking at the base of the square has made the integration of service mechanisms unifying one of the objectives of the project. In this way the elevators, stairways exits, and ventilation, etc. are plastically integrated, playing with the elements of the towers and the pergola, which have been planned to integrate the lighting. This same lighting allows creating different environments, dynamic spaces, spaces of communication, some with more light, others soft lighting with shades of rest and tranquility. The public space has to pamper the user.

Based on the existing parking lot an artificial topography is created, formalized by the intersection of two pyramids, which merges with the Segre River and connects with the sidewalks of the surrounding streets with inclined planes, ramps or stairs, thereby continuing urban routes.

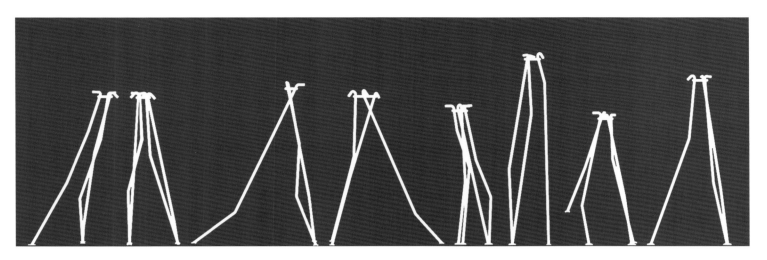

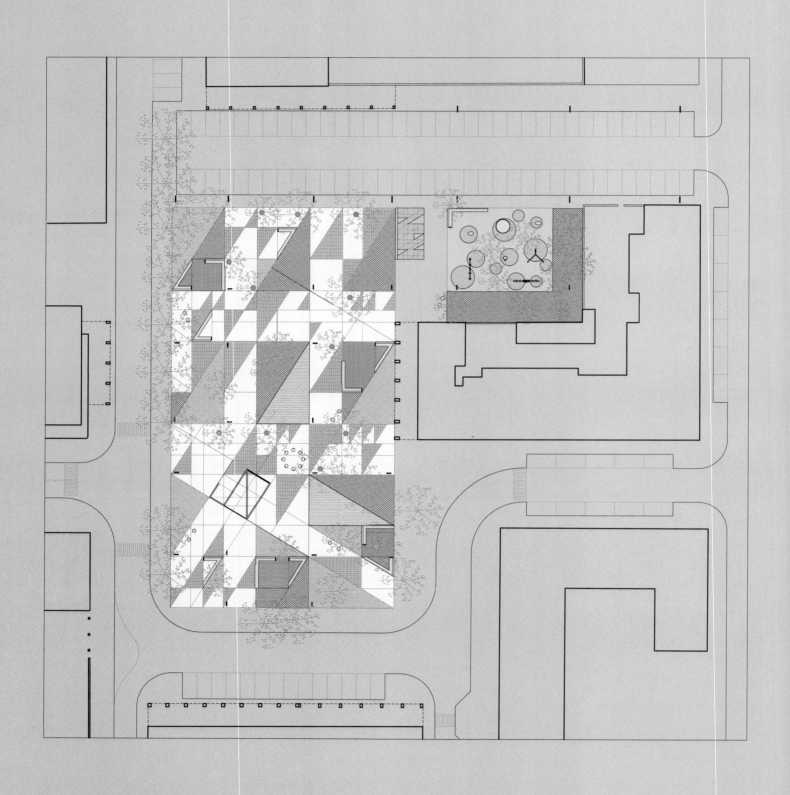

Design Agency: Labics	Location: Milan, Italy
Designer: Maria Claudia Clemente, Francesco Isidori, Gaia Maria Lombardo	Area: 6, 200 m²
Photography: Luigi Filetici	

Fontana Square in Quinto de Stampi

General Description:

The urban design for a public square in Rozzano, a suburb of Milan, offers the local community a flexible and shared outdoor space.

Design Concept:

The aim of this project was to create a new, flexible and welcoming landscape for the local neighborhood which would satisfy the community's complex and continuously changing needs. Labics' intention was to make a space which would also trigger new, unplanned uses while retaining a strong local identity. A public consultation helped the municipality to define a very precise brief, accommodating the many different requirements and aspirations of the local community.

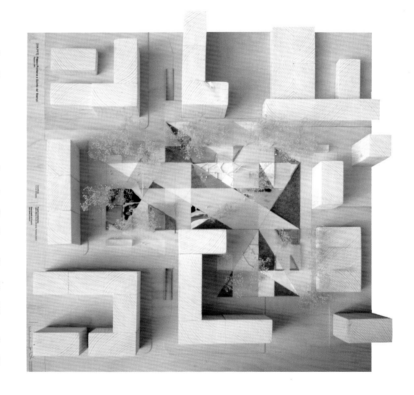

Design Details:

The geometrical pattern of the landscape is based on a dense grid of "golden rectangles" (i.e. rectangles with side lengths in the golden ratio of 1:1.6), with the dimensions of these determining every element of the square from the planting to the paving. A system of triangular shapes inside this orthogonal pattern helps to define the various natural and artificial surface treatments within the landscape, which include water, stone, lawn, shrubs and planted beds. A variety of trees, including cherries, pears, birches and acacias, has been planted to ensure a changing display of blossom and color throughout the year. The paving is composed of a variety of materials ranging from local stone to iroko timber and concrete. To emphasize the lightly undulating topography of the

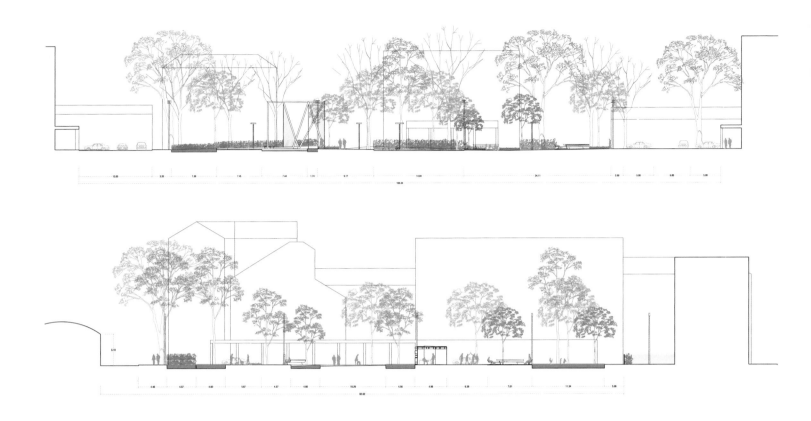

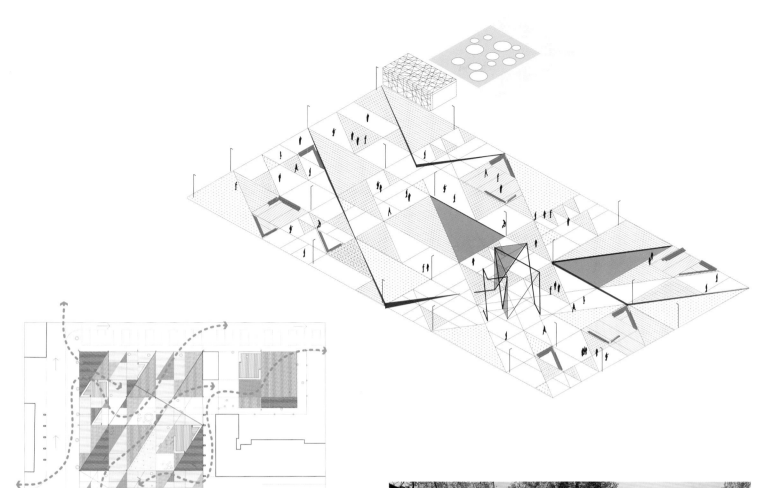

square, the landscape has been artificially "bended" to create a dynamic space. A contemporary sculpture which acts as a gateway to the neighborhood, benches and a pavilion/info point populate the square, providing spaces for play, relaxation and interaction.

A system of triangular shapes inside this
orthogonal pattern helps to define the
various natural and artificial surface
treatments within the landscape, which
include water, stone, lawn, shrubs
and planted beds.

N

0 10 30 50 100 M

Design Agency: Mayslits Kassif Architects

Designer: Ganit Mayslits Kassif, Udi Kassif,

Oren Ben Avraham, Galila Yavin,

Michal Ilan, Maor Roytman

Photography: Adi Brande, Daniela Orvin, Galia Kronfeld

Location: Tel Aviv port, Israel

Area: 55,000 m²

Tel Aviv Port Public Space Regeneration

General Description:

Situated on one of Israel's most breathtaking waterfronts, the Tel Aviv Port was plagued with neglect since 1965, when its primary use as an operational docking port was abandoned. Mayslits Kassif Architects made the completed public space development project,

managed to restore this unique part of the city, and turned it into a prominent, vivacious urban landmark.

Design Concept:

The architects viewed the project as a unique opportunity to construct a public space which challenges the common contrast between private and public development, and suggests a new agenda of hospitality for collective open spaces.

Being a new urban landmark which revives the city's waterfront, the project became a trigger for a series of public space projects along Tel Aviv's shoreline which altogether revolutionize the city's connection to its waterfront.

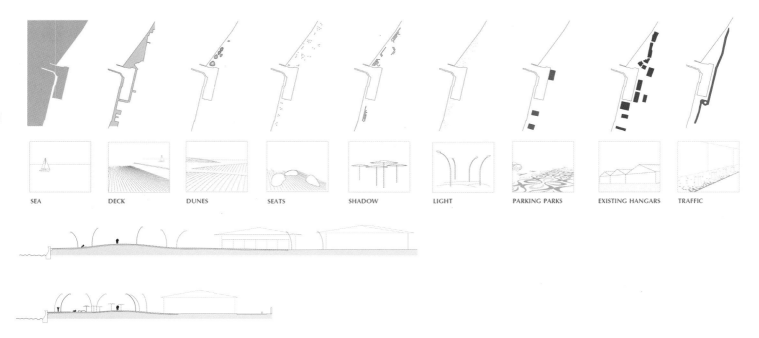

SEA   DECK   DUNES   SEATS   SHADOW   LIGHT   PARKING PARKS   EXISTING HANGARS   TRAFFIC

©Adi Brande

Design Details:

The design introduces an extensive undulating, non-hierarchical surface, that acts both as a reflection of the mythological dunes on which the port was built, and as an open invitation to free interpretations and unstructured activities. Various public and social initiatives — from spontaneous rallies to artistic endeavors and public acts of solidarity — are now drawn to this unique urban platform, indicating the project's success in reinventing the port as a vibrant public sphere.

©Daniela Orvin

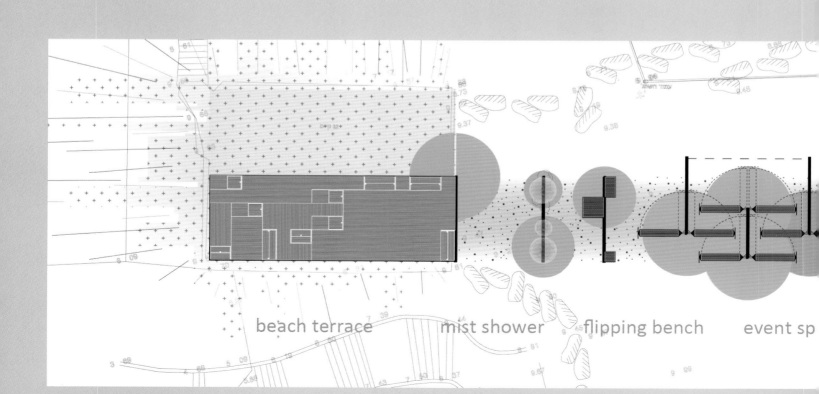

beach terrace   mist shower   flipping bench   event sp

Design Agency: *Derman Verbakel Architecture*

Photography: *Yuval Tebol*

Location: *Bat-Yam, Israel*

Area: *500 m²*

On the Way to the Sea

General Description:

The project transforms the space that lies between the city and the sea to a place of its own rather than an in-between passage. A series of frames carefully positioned between city edge to sea shore host public activities, creating a new use for this in-between space.

Design Concept:

In the gap between city and sea, the project encourages collective and individual interactions that range from urban events to beach activities.

picnic area   patio   room   salon   balcony   ramp

Design Details:

A series of fixed frames containing movable elements creates a basic infrastructure in which users have the freedom to alter the urban space and fit it to their own private uses. Starting at the city edge, visitors can start engaging in the space through an entrance ramp at the individual scale, leading to a balcony facing the street, followed by an "unfolded" living room with elements that can be used as walking surface, table or chair. Starting from this more intimate apartment layout that faces the street, the installation then transforms towards the beach into a series of more public spaces such as "picnic on the lawn" — a flexible structure with movable benches and tables turning around an axis, allowing for different seating arrangements and shaded "urban rooms" that can be used for birthday parties or other social events. At the interface between the project and the beach, an open terrace offers views to the sea, providing shade and reclined seating facing the horizon. Together, the elements create a micro-climate where people can meet, play, eat, talk or just hang out, thereby producing a platform for a wide range of possible interactions, from daily uses to special events.

Design Agency: FoRM Associates

Photography: Rhys Wynne, Web Aviation, FoRM Associates

Location: Manchester, UK

Area: 3, 850 m²

Trafford Wharf Promenade

General Description:

The new promenade designed by FoRM Associates is located in Salford Quays, an area which has been for a long time on the industrial outskirts of Manchester and now is becoming a vital creative hub on the River Irwell.

Design Concept:

With the adjoining new Media City foot bridge by Wilkinson Eyre Architects, the quayside delivers an important new strategic circulation loop in the Quays, a key regeneration zone in Greater Manchester. The loop helps to transform the experience of walking in the area through linking Media City UK — the new home of the BBC, with the IWMN, Manchester United Stadium and Lowry Arts Centre.

Design Details:

Trafford Wharf Promenade in front of Imperial War Museum North proved to be one missing piece in the puzzle. It acts also as a new setting for Daniel Libeskind's Imperial War Museum North, which has previously been accessed only via a parking lot and

had little relationship to the waterfront. Trafford Wharf Promenade reoriented the building onto the water with a new entrance that already now admits over 50% of the museum visitors.

FoRM's design of the quayside plays with convex and concave geometries, creating an imaginative public realm that contemplates the striking forms of Imperial War Museum North. It has quickly become a place for gathering and informal events for the museum, as well as an "auditorium" from which to watch the river and the buzz of the Media City UK on the other bank.

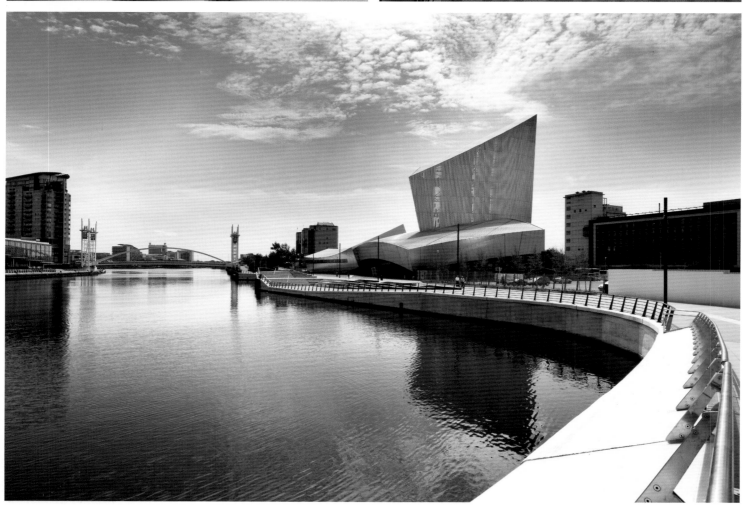

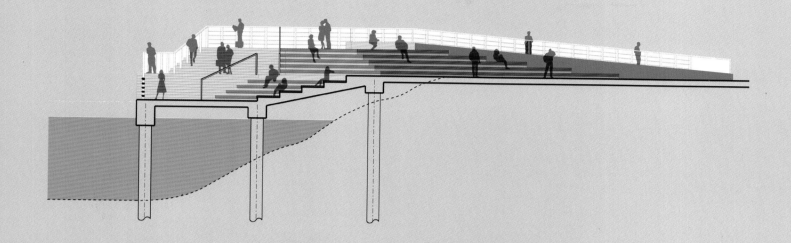

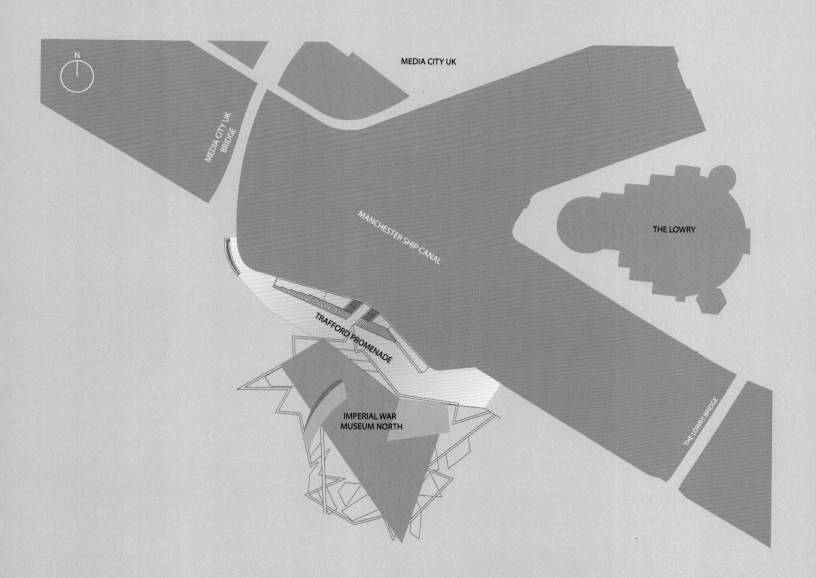

MEDIA CITY UK

MEDIA CITY UK BRIDGE

MANCHESTER SHIP CANAL

THE LOWRY

TRAFFORD PROMENADE

THE LOWRY BRIDGE

IMPERIAL WAR MUSEUM NORTH

N

Design Agency: *Guallart Architects*

Photography: *Adrià Goula*

Location: *Taiwan, China*

Area: *4, 500 m²*

Keelung Port

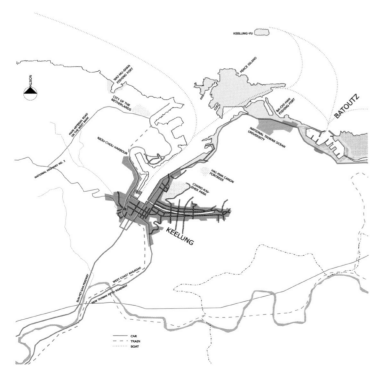

General Description:

Keelung is the port of Taipei, the capital of the island of Taiwan. Located 30 km to the north of the capital, it is one of the most important container ports in Asia. Keelung has all the vitality of a major port, with one of the most bustling night-time markets in the Far East and an extensive and multifarious central commercial area adjoining the port.

Design Concept:

In order to promote the urbanism of Keelung, to establish relationships between the different pieces that make up the central space of the city, to identify the characteristics of a new central public space for the city with which the citizens of Keelung could identify, the project focuses on improving the urban quality of Keelung and has emerged with notable success from the quantitative phase of its urban development.

Design Details:

There are three proposals for the construction of the project. Among them, the third one, on which the construction project is based, assumed a fixed coastline, centering the design on the creation of a dynamic line between the urban edge and the platform, reworking ideas developed in previous projects. In this case, having analyzed the functioning of the various activities that come together here, the scheme proposes a pergola that provides a covered walkway extending from the commercial zone to the station, dynamically expanding this structure by way of the wooden platform. This pergola, created with a linear pattern like the tentacular fronds of a marine

plant, is folded both vertically and horizontally to generate rest spaces on the seafront and to spell out the word K-E-E-L-U-N-G on the urban front. This new timber platform will thus act as an icon similar to those ferry terminals in which the name of the port is eye-catchingly displayed. The timber platform also has a garden of wooden "rocks" that will be replicated in the Ocean Plaza in Batoutz. In this case, the traditional Oriental rock gardens are materially transformed to become folds in the surface of the public space, inviting people to relate to them physically in various ways; a similar appropriation has been made of the outcrops of volcanic rock on the neighboring coast.

The new amenities and leisure spaces, the effective pedestrian link between the different urban sectors and the bridge itself constitute the bases on which centrality will be reinforced by the intensity and dynamism of the human relationships it accommodates.

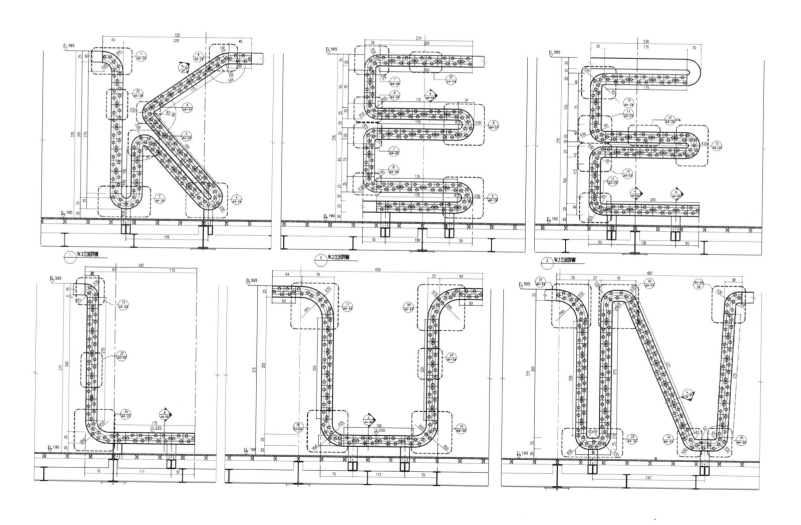

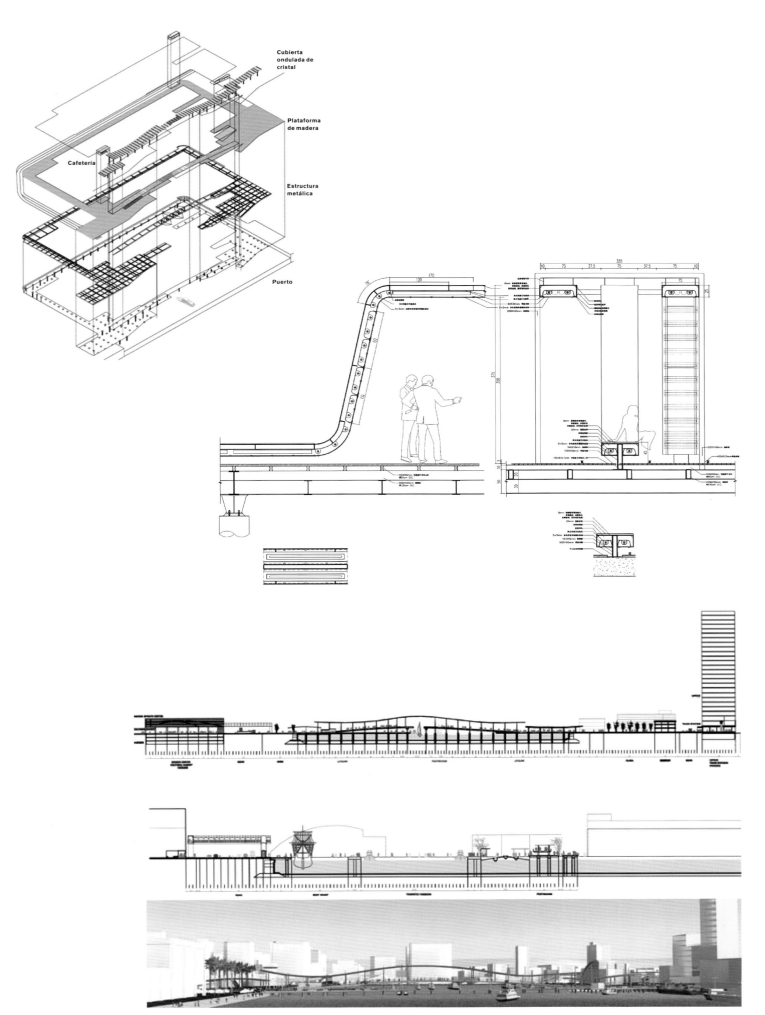

Cubierta
ondulada de
cristal

Plataforma
de madera

Cafetería

Estructura
metálica

Puerto

261

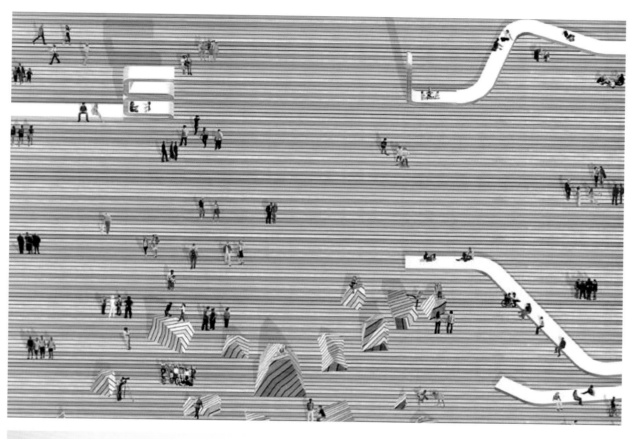

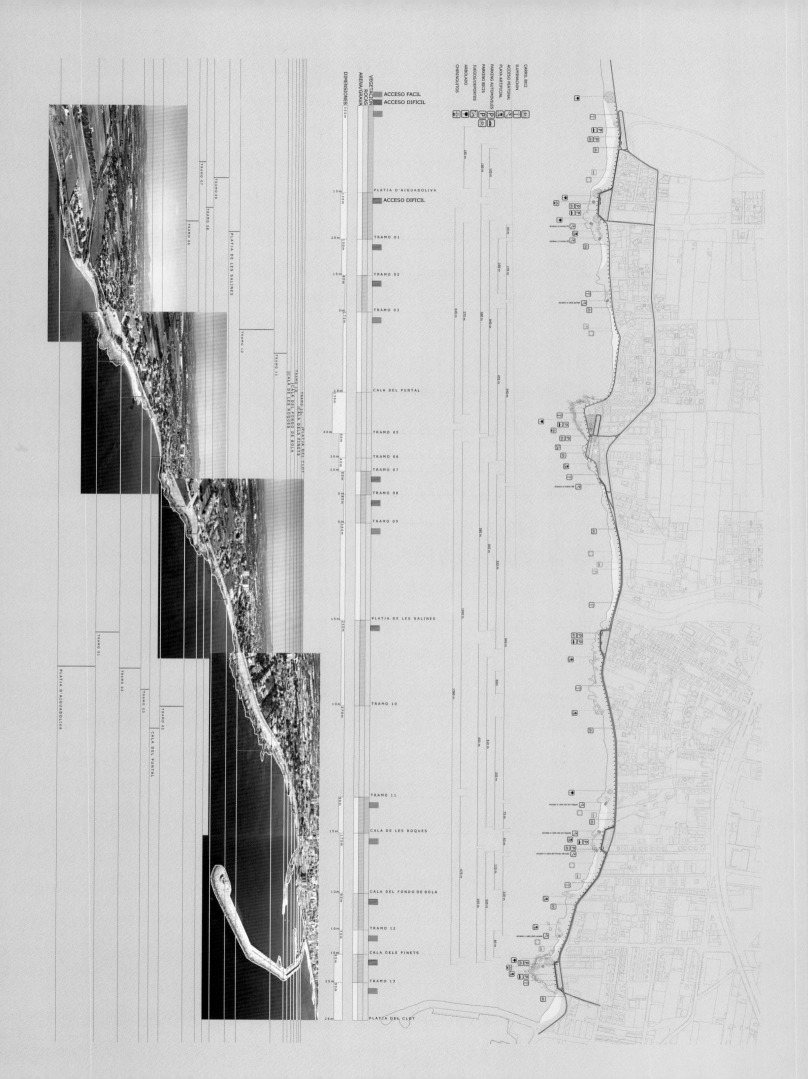

Design Agency: *Guallart Architects*

Photography: *Laura Cantarella, Nuria Diaz*

Location: *Vinaròs, Spain*

Area: *1 km (length of Microcoasts Vinaròs)*

Microcoasts Vinaròs

General Description:

Vinaròs is a town on the Mediterranean coast of Spain, near the delta of the river Ebro. Its southern shore, the location of the project, is a succession of coves and promontories on a terrain composed of strata of easily fractured conglomerate rocks. The length of the coastline and the surface area of the municipality are constant changing as a result of the action of the sea, which causes continual land slippage and erosion. This zone has been developed with detached houses on small plots.

Design Concept:

The project inspires people's interest to the new micro-coasts. The relationship of the size, orientation and location of the platform and the number and social profile of the people using them is interesting in terms of the socialization of the space.

Design Details:

The project aimed to establish a mechanism to measure the coast, on the basis of the creation of hexagonal timber platforms with a constant length of side based on the scale of the human body. These micro-coasts are organized to form islands of variable sizes, located by the sea. The platforms are composed of two different pieces, one flat, the other with micro topography, which serve to generate surfaces that can be perfectly flat or partially or fully folded. Their positioning on the coast is determined by criteria of access to the sea and interaction with the dynamic line of the original coast.

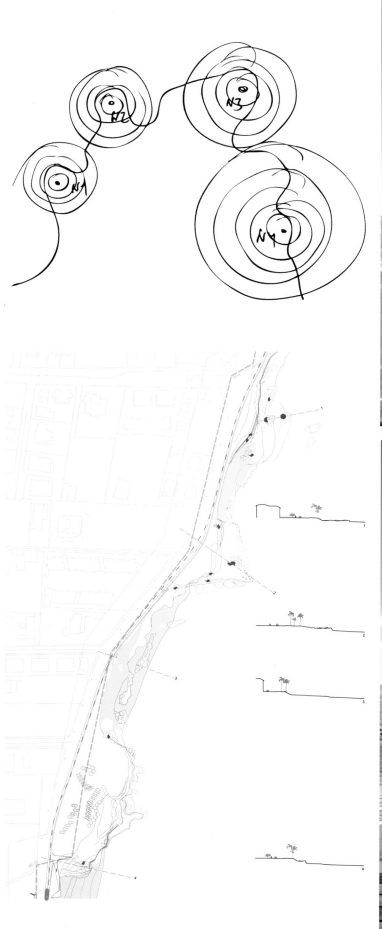

DIMENSIÓN GENERAL
DE LAS PIEZAS

ESTRUCTURA:
CRITERIOS

ENSAMBLAJE
ENTRE PIEZAS

COLOCACIÓN + ORIENTACIÓN
DE LAS LAMAS DE MADERA

EJEMPLO DE TRAMAS QUE SE CONSIGUEN CON
UNA SOLA PIEZA (sin variación)

Apoyo principal

Estructura principal
Estructura secundaria

Estructura principal
Estructura secundaria

Planta

Planta

Alzado

Sección

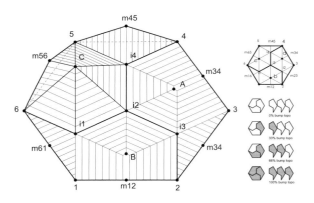

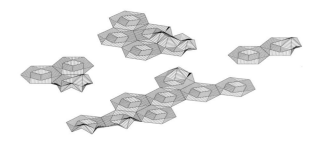

These micro coasts are organized to form islands of variable sizes, located where there is rock in close proximity to the sea, providing areas for people to enjoy a nice sunbath.

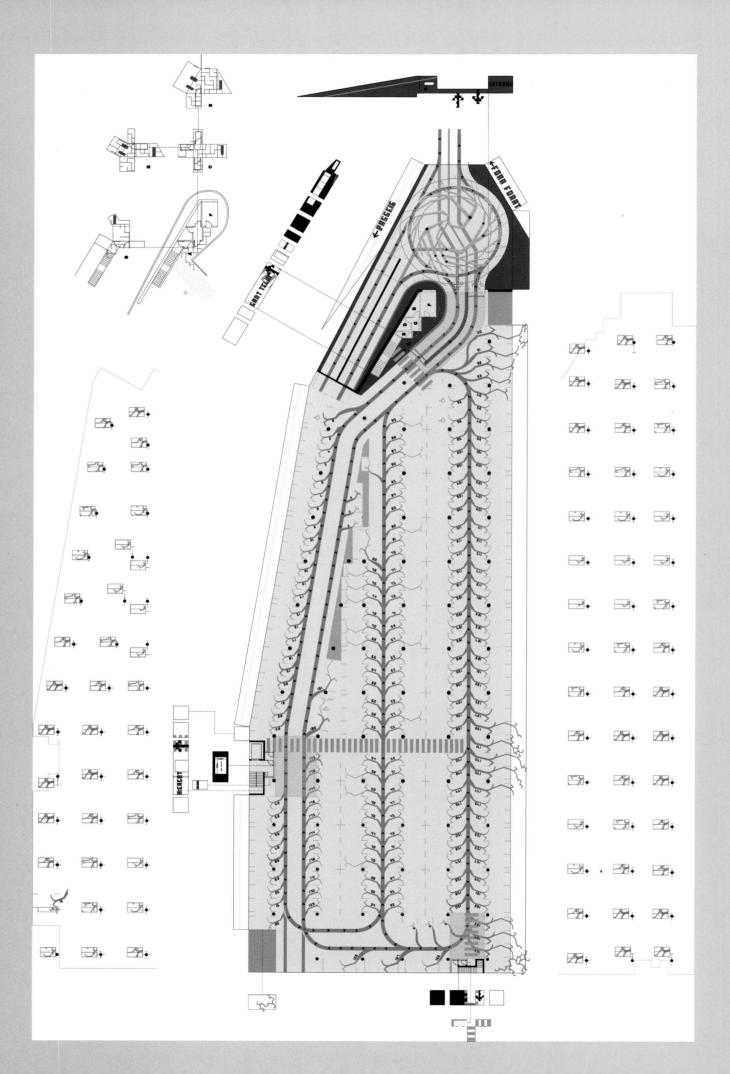

Vinaròs Promenade

General Description:

The promenade is today a place of great urban vitality, occupied mainly by cars, which coexists with seafood restaurants, an open-air auditorium for orchestral and choral concerts and open-air film screenings, regular street markets and events throughout the year, frequented by people on their way to and from the beach.

Design Concept:

The reform of the seafront promenade, as the interface between the center of the town and the sea, offered a great opportunity for a public initiative to define the desired standards of urban quality for future growth.

Design Details:

The main decision here was to transform the entire promenade into an area for pedestrian use, in order to take full advantage of the place's potential tourists and civic potential, restricting vehicle access for loading and unloading to certain times of the day, and allowing freer access out of season. The structure of the town's road system is such that traffic in the part closest to the port could

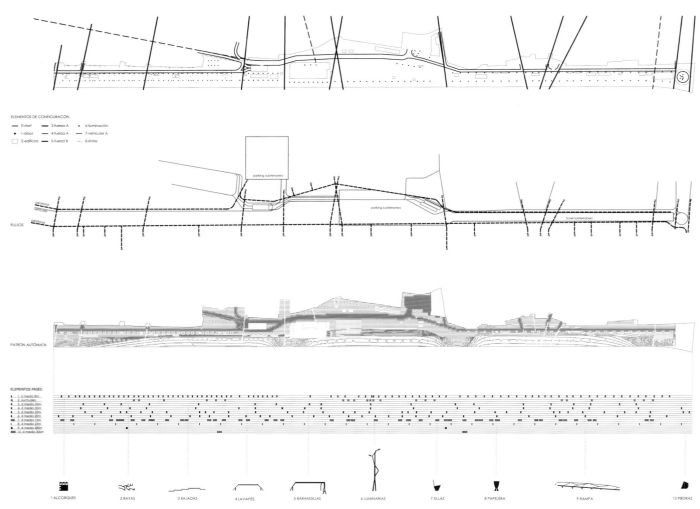

be routed behind the buildings on the streets parallel to the promenade. However, the absence of any such parallel streets in the central and northern sectors prompted the decision to construct a tunnel between the end of the promenade and the 250-place car park to be laid out beneath the central plaza. This car park will be connected with others in or under adjacent squares to create a real underground mobility network that allows cars to drive in from the outskirts to the center of the town and park close to the beach and the seafront promenade. It was also decided to eliminate the concrete wall separating the beach from the promenade to enable the whole area to be perceived as a continuous space composed of a variety of materials, from the sand of the artificial beach to the cenia stone from a local quarry. Another significant decision was that the promenade, which at present has an irregular topography, should have a constant level that would set off its eight hundred meter horizontal line against the natural line of the sea's horizon. This serves to resolve the difference in level between the beach and the promenade by means of a system of tiers that can be occupied in a variety of ways.

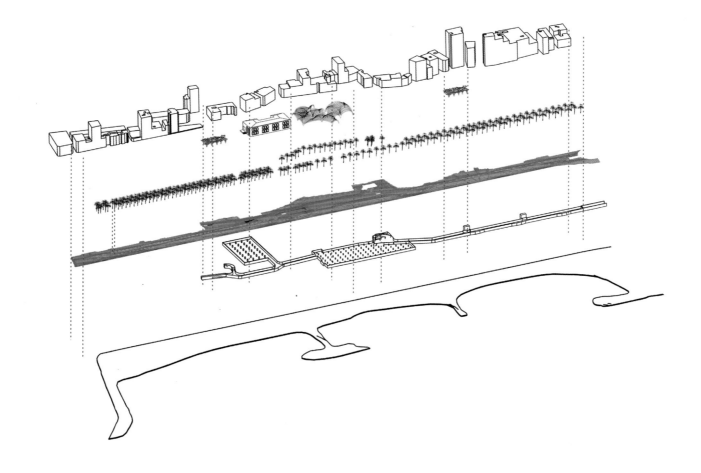

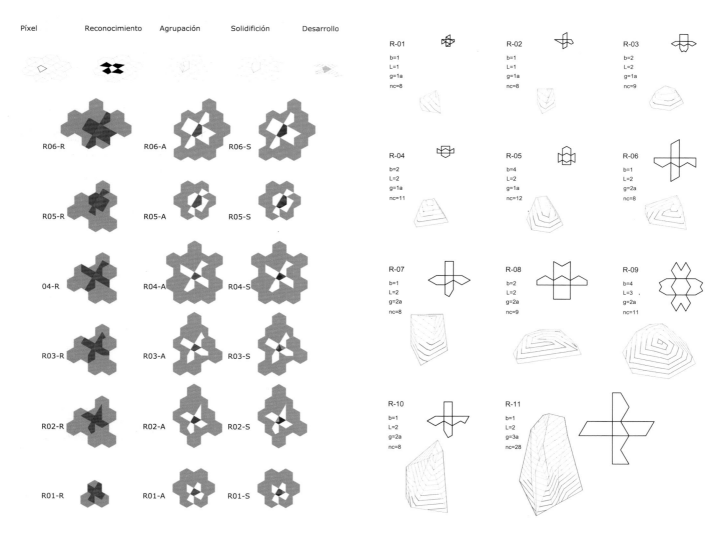

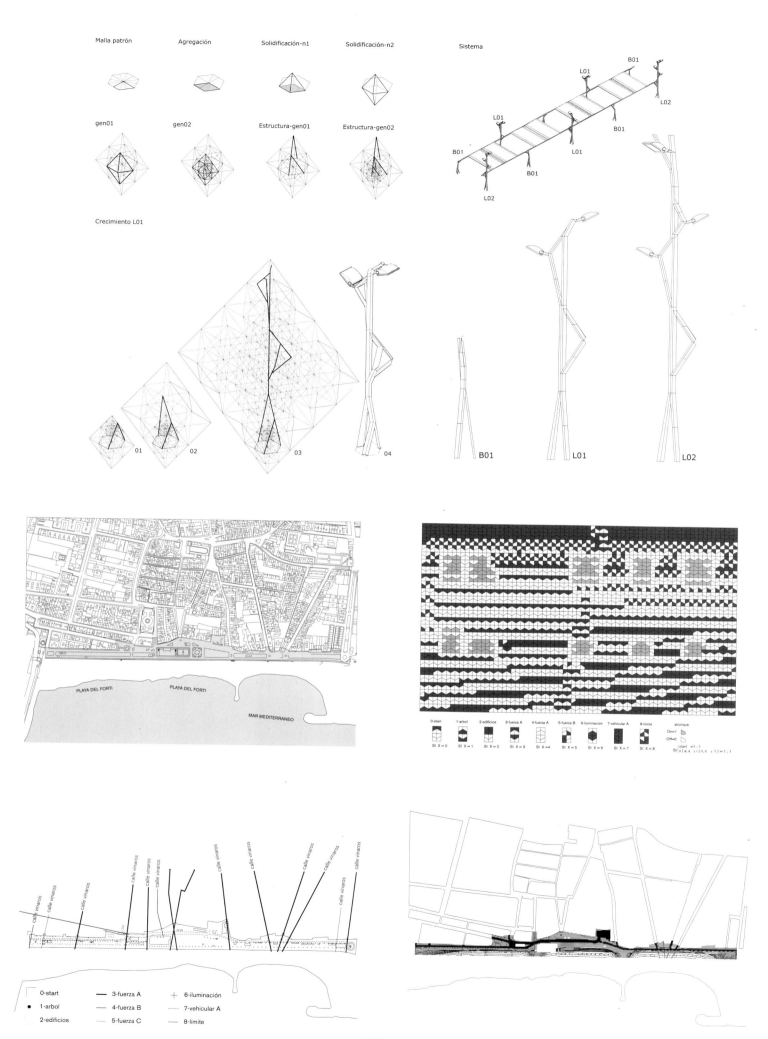

Malla patrón   Agregación   Solidificación-n1   Solidificación-n2   Sistema

B01

L01

B01

L01

B01

L01

L02

L02

gen01   gen02   Estructura-gen01   Estructura-gen02

Crecimiento L01

01   02   03   04

B01   L01   L02

PLAYA DEL FORTI   PLAYA DEL FORTI

MAR MEDITERRANEO

0-start	1-arbol	2-edificios	3-fuerza A	4-fuerza A	5-fuerza B	6-iluminacion	7-vehicular A	8-limite	alcorque
SI X = 0	SI X = 1	SI X = 2	SI X = 3	SI X = 4	SI X = 5	SI X = 6	SI X = 7	SI X = 8	On=1 Off=0

$x\{a,a \text{ s.t } n,n \text{ s.t}\} = 1 : 1$

calle vinaros (repeated)

0-start	3-fuerza A	6-iluminación
1-arbol	4-fuerza B	7-vehicular A
2-edificios	5-fuerza C	8-limite

275

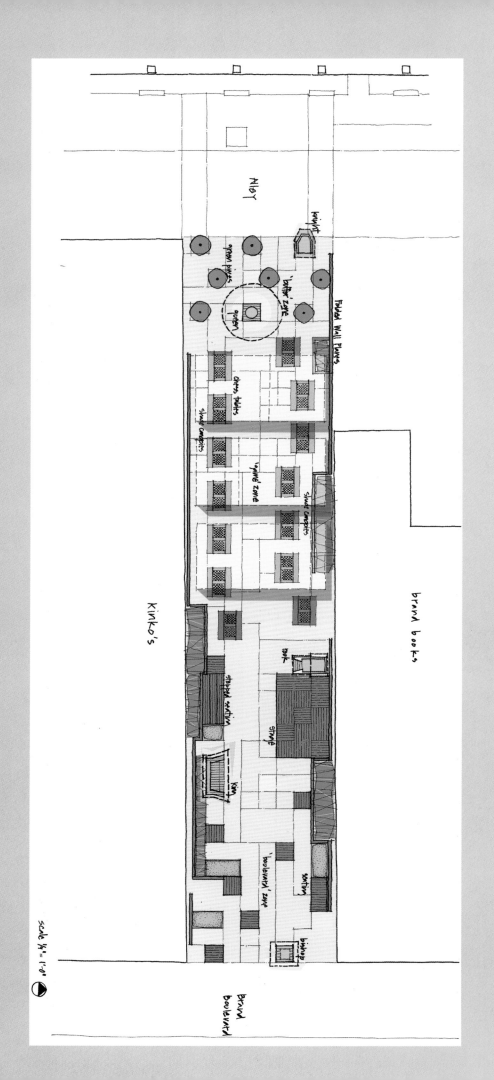

Alley

knight

green pieces

'buffer' zone

queen

Folded Wall Plains

chess tablets

shade canopies

'living' zone

shade canopies

rook

stripped section

stage

King

'boulevard' zone

seating

bishop

Kinko's

brand books

Brand
boulevard

scale ¼" = 1'-0"

Design Agency: *Rios Clementi Hale Studios*

Designer: *Mark Rios, Frank Clementi, Anthony Paradowski, Samantha Harris, Ola May*

Photography: *Tom Bonner*

Location: *Glendale, USA*

Area: *418 m²*

Chess Park

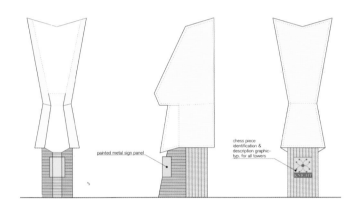

painted metal sign panel

chess piece
identification &
description graphic-
typ. for all towers

KNIGHT

General Description:

The site sandwiched between two retail stores on Brand Boulevard's center village, formerly served as a pathway from a city parking garage to a theater and surrounding shops. The aim was to transform a city passageway into a thriving, community-oriented chess park where players, the local community, and passersby can collectively participate in gamesmanship and festivities.

Design Concept:

The city of the project desired an affordable, low-maintenance plan that was easily executable while bringing a wholesome, lively meeting place to the city's main drag. It wanted to provide a clean, safe environment for the local chess club and other participants to call home.

Design Details:

To transform the rectangular space into a chess park, the designers researched the game's rich history and based the design program on its playing rituals, strategies, and lore. While every detail and nuance is derived from the tradition and lexicon of the game, the park's entire design is patterned after strategic movements made in chess.

In proclamation of the park's intent, the designers created five playful light towers fashioned after the shape of chess pieces. The base of each 28-foot-high lantern is constructed from Trex, a recycled plastic and wood lumber product, and topped with white synthetic canvas formed in the shape of an abstracted chess piece. The light towers emit a warm glow and are strategically placed around the park, inspiring creativity and intellectual challenge.

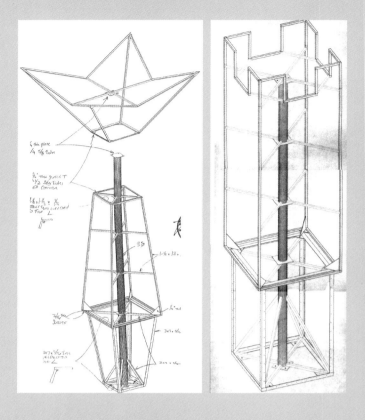

While the towers bring an iconic presence to the park, they also provide significant lighting and space to help solve the park's functional needs. The space is organized into three zones — the boulevard zone, gaming zone, and buffer zone — which give clarity to the different design elements.

The Bishop Tower stands at the entrance of the Brand Boulevard zone. Its role as a messenger is marked by the base, which carries the park entrance signage. Nearby, the King Tower sits as a giant, story-telling throne where community members can engage in outreach activities such as performances and book readings. Across the throne is a platform where musicians, actors, and artists can gather together and showcase their talents. A gray Trex wall folds up behind the platform to create a backdrop for performances. The Rook Tower, in the shape of an abstracted castle, is next to the stage, providing storage and technical support for events. Low concrete benches with Trex tops provide seating for local workers to enjoy their lunches or coffee breaks.

The park's center area is designated as the gaming zone where players congregate around the 16 concrete chess tables that feature inlaid black and white tile chess boards. The powerful Queen Tower presides over this area and stands as a symbol for the Glendale Chess Club. The Knight Tower stands as a sentry in the buffer zone near the alleyway, vigilantly protecting the park.

The two long borders of the park are lined with a series of screen walls of varying sizes, which are made from the same gray Trex material as the other design elements. While providing seating, lighting, and display opportunities, the screen walls also offset the scale of the tall buildings that flank the sides of the passageway. The designers planted the park's borders with lush, low maintenance shrubbery and white flowering perennials. Cypress trees provide a buffer to the alley.

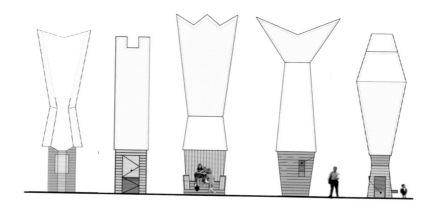

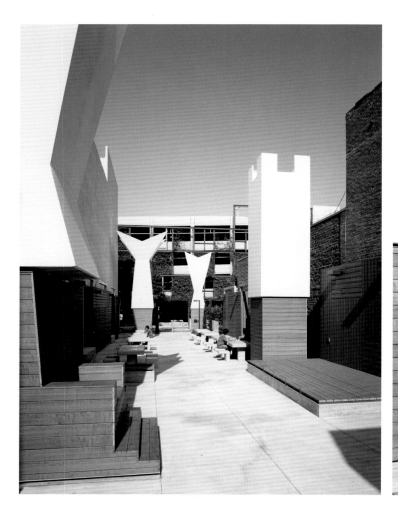

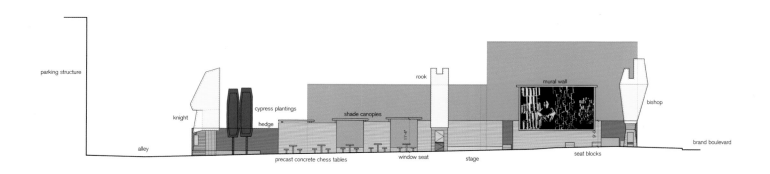

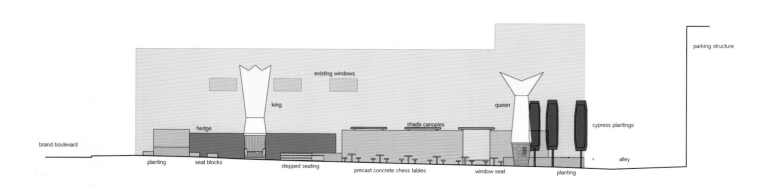

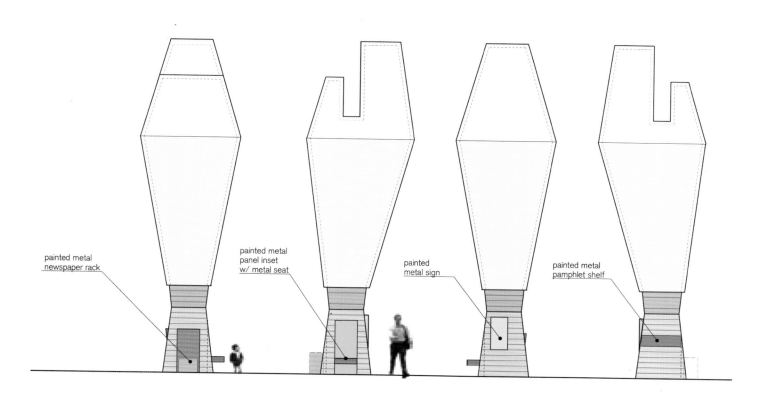

painted metal
newspaper rack

painted metal
panel inset
w/ metal seat

painted
metal sign

painted metal
pamphlet shelf

283

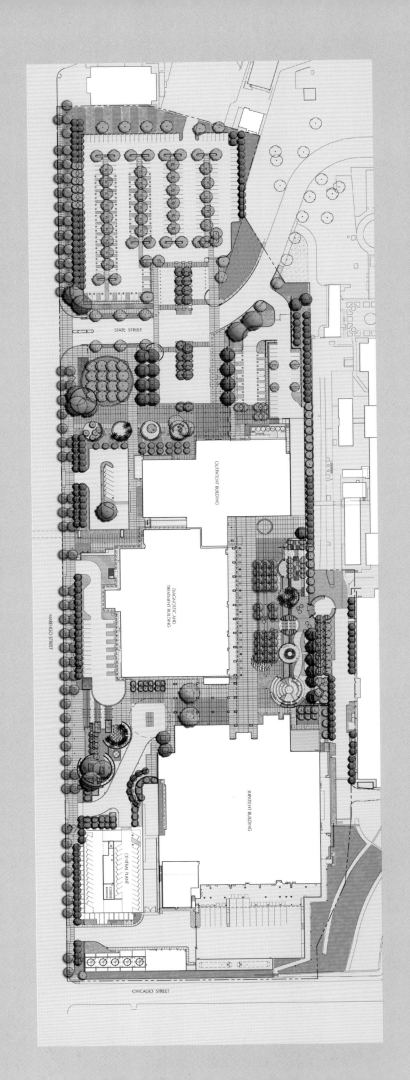

STATE STREET

MARENGO STREET

OUTPATIENT BUILDING

DIAGNOSTIC AND
TREATMENT BUILDING

INPATIENT BUILDING

CENTRAL PLANT

CHICAGO STREET

Design Agency: *Rios Clementi Hale Studios*	Photography: *Tom Bonner*
Designer: *Mark W. Rios, Tony Paradowski, Mark Tessier,*	Location: *Los Angeles, USA*
Mike Cheng, Samantha Harris, Carolyn Sumida, Melendrez	Area: *80, 937 m²*
Design Partners, *Lauren Melendrez, Tony Chacon*	

284-289

LAC + USC
Medical Center

General Description:

In conceiving the landscape architecture for the new Los Angeles County + University of Southern California Medical Center (LAC + USC) site, Rios Clementi Hale Studios used large, bold, geometric patterns abstracted from regional history and geology.

Design Concept:

The design re-interprets and integrates elements and patterns from the new building and existing site throughout the more than 20-acre campus. The result is a fluid and engaging conversation between structure, landscape, and community.

Design Details:

Rios Clementi Hale Studios' extensive site work encompasses automobile and pedestrian circulation systems, entry plazas, pedestrian thoroughfares and plazas, gardens, and the overall development and patterning of hardscape and planting. The design delineates a distinct identity for each individual element and its functional needs, and unifies them with a master plan that organically fits the building to its site.

An animated juxtaposition of circular and rectilinear shapes blankets the tiered ground plane like a Mexican tapestry, giving way to a mosaic of paving patterns and site features. Elements include a long grove of oak trees set diagonal to a curved lawn amphitheater — a ribbon-like ramp leads to a pedestrian walkway above.

Refreshing tree bosques, colored concrete, sand-colored decomposed granite hardscape, drought-tolerant underplantings and shrubs, and seating areas and gardens of various sizes play into the overall pattern.

The feeling is open and spacious, yet comfortably interconnected.

The landscape architecture further addresses 100 feet of elevation change across the 20 acres. At the site's lowest level, abstract wave-like patterns run through the concrete paving surface. At the high point, columnar Canary Island pine trees evoke the mountain peaks and vistas surrounding Los Angeles.

Throughout, graceful lines, ramps, stairs, plazas, and walkways traverse the pedestrian-friendly topography.

Rios Clementi Hale Studios also designed a line of concrete and metal site furnishings expressly for LAC + USC's outdoor environs. The pieces are composed of a system of repetitive forms and echo the overriding site design. Examples include the curved concrete benches that ring a series of circular meditation gardens, each planted in a distinct fashion. Nearby, a round, plant-free seating plaza is embedded with a ground design suggesting a meditative labyrinth. Other areas feature rows of rectangular concrete benches detailed with a slatted-wood treatment on the seating surfaces.

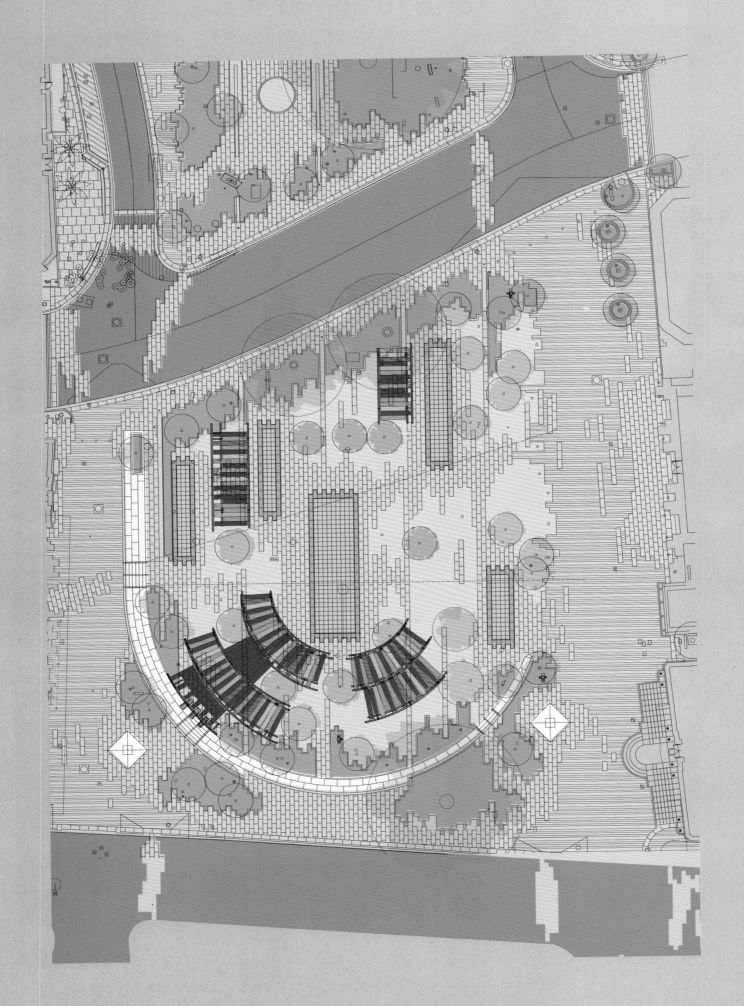

Design Agency: *Rios Clementi Hale Studios*

Designer: *Mark Rios, Samantha Harris, Chris Adamick*

Photography: *Nick Simonite*

Location: *San Antonio, USA*

Area: *6, 273 m²*

Main Plaza Shade Structures

General Description:

The historic Main Plaza is a heavily programmed public space located in the heart of the City of San Antonio. During construction of the first phase of the new landscape begun in 2006, the old-growth Red Oak trees that had been providing deep shade in the plaza were damaged and subsequently died. Now,

the first-phase plaza design was a monochromatic beige landscape in a city known for its vibrant colors and the task for the shade canopies is multifold: provide shade while the newly planted trees grow, provide color to tie into the local culture, and create visual interest while not impeding the crucial view of the Cathedral from the Riverwalk portal.

Design Concept:

Rios Clementi Hale Studios was commissioned to create canopies to provide shade while young replacement trees grow in. The design for the shade canopies takes inspiration from San Antonio's handmade tradition and rich multi-cultural and ethnic history. The aesthetic character of the canopies was conceived as a woven ribbon through the trees with a structural system that blends in with the site and footings that disappear directly into the earth supporting a light and airy series of colored bands that float away from the steel structures and stand out against the green leaves and blue sky.

Design Details:

Ojos de Dios (woven God's Eyes), papel picado colored perforated paper craftwork, and indigenous textile design provide the inspiration for overlapping bands of color and sculptural angles, while the bipartite form experienced under the trellises and archways at the Mission San Jose informed the quality of the spaces beneath. Each canopy creates an average 800-square-foot sized area of shade using the colorful fabric bands woven together overhead in an array of sculptural forms. They provide temporal visual interest that shifts depending on the location of the viewer as well as beautiful shadow patterns that alter with the location of the sun.

The innovative individual tilted panel system design provides several benefits, making them both economically and environmentally sustainable. They are easily and inexpensively maintained; if one fabric panel is damaged, just that one rectilinear panel will need replacement and its color need not match that of its neighbors due to the multi-colored arrangement. The panel system reduces wind load on the structure, allowing enough breeze to blow through to keep the shaded air circulating and cool. The panel angles provide the densest shade at the height of summer when it's most needed, and allow more sunlight to filter through in winter. Movable tables and chairs allow people to sit in the most comfortable spots at any given moment and congregate as they wish. Specific programmatic shade zones were chosen for casual seating as well as for optimal locations for performance.

The steel canopy structures were designed as a kit of parts with individual components and assembly details worked out in advance at the local fabrication shop. Pre-fabricated structural joints and details were designed to make for quick and simple assembly on site, and local fabrication reduced transportation costs both economically and environmentally. Off-the-shelf parts were used wherever possible, reducing costs and making maintenance of details.

293

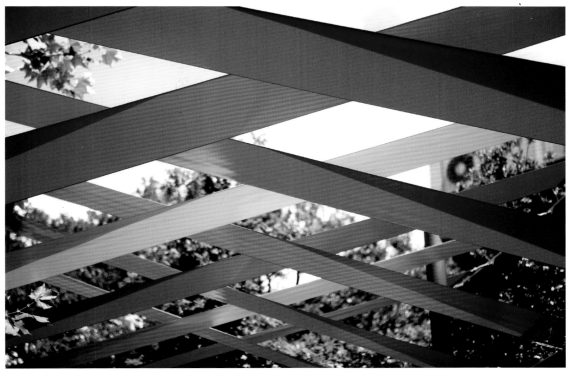

The beautiful canopies are naturally integrated into the surrounding like a huge tree that offers shade to passersby.

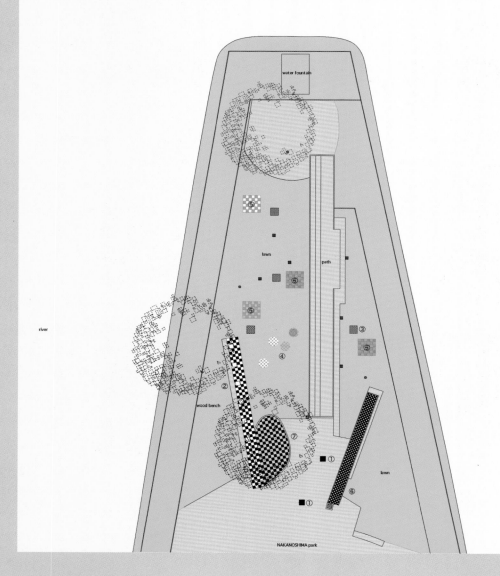

water fountain

river

lawn

path

wood bench

river

②

⑤

⑤

⑤

③

⑤

④

⑦

b

■①

■①

⑥

lawn

NAKANOSHIMA park

①. boardgame tower
②. mirror boardgame (on the bench)
③. box boardgame (on the lawn)
④. round boardgame (on the manhole cover)
⑤. picnic checker sheet
⑥. checker path
⑦. checker garden

Design Agency: Kansai University, TOFU architect

Designer: Hikaru Kinoshita, TOFU, Yuji Tamai

Photography: Yohei Sasakura

Location: Osaka, Japan

Area: 1, 350 m²

Osaka Board Game Park

General Description:

In end of October 2011, Aqua Metropolis Osaka 2011 Festival was hold in Nakanoshima Park and its surroundings for 9 days. Various art installations brought out the waterside attractiveness. Osaka Board Game Park is one of these art installations at the east end of Nakanoshima Park.

Design Concept:

The design team aimed to make the project simple, low cost and to create a beautiful and attractive park in a new urban and landscape design. The project demonstrated how to enrich public space.

Design Details:

The design team designed and built the checkers made of various materials (paper, cardboard, cloth, vinyl sheet flooring, wood, tile, stone and stainless steel) based on the existing context of the park. They set game-boards in various ways on the grass and benches in the park. More people can play Othello & Chess and enjoy the comfortable time and space with our board game.

mirror board game

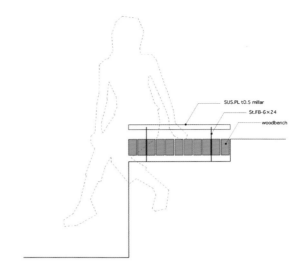

SUS.PL t0.5 millar
St.FB-6×24
woodbench

round board game

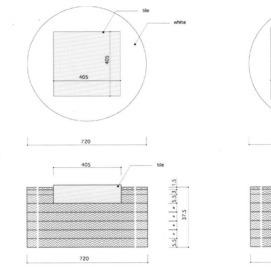

tile
white
405
405
720
405
tile
1.5
5.5
5.5
3
37.5
720

tile
white
455
455
720
455
tile
1.5
5.5
5.5
3
37.5
720

board game tower

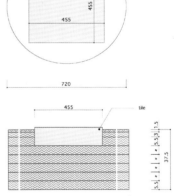

corrugated cardboard
244.5
244.5
500
500

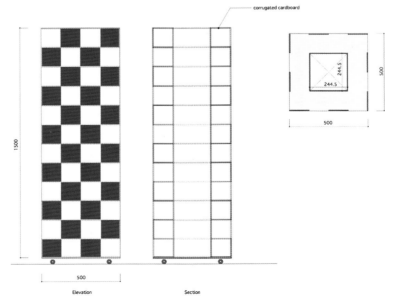

1500
500
Elevation
Section

THEATER

HOTEL

MISERY HILL

FORBES STREET

GRAND CANAL

N

Design Agency: Martha Schwartz Partners

Designer: Martha Schwartz

Photography: Martha Schwartz Partners, Time Crocker

Location: Dublin, Ireland

Area: 10, 000 m²

Grand Canal Square

General Description:

Grand Canal Square is the major public open space in the Dublin Docklands Development area. It is located on Grand Canal in Dublin and forms the focal point of the area.

Design Concept:

In this setting dominated by contemporary architectural expression, MSP has created a public space that offers color and dynamism to Dublin's open spaces.

Design Details:

Due to its cultural celebrity setting, a scheme with a central red carpet has been developed that leads from the theater out onto the canal and vice versa. A green carpet connects the new hotel to the office development area. The red carpet is paved in a newly– developed, bright red resin/ glass material. Red–glowing, angled light sticks that mimic the "bustle" on the red carpet accent the grand walkway. The green carpet has a calmer expression and offers ample seating on the edges of planters of various heights. The planters, extruded polygons of the green carpet, are planted with marsh vegetation as a reminder of the historic wetland area of this site. Some offer immaculate lawns for lingering and enjoying the spectacular setting. Pushing out of the plaza is a water feature of randomly stacked green marble that is overflowing with bubbling water.

© Time Crocker

The square is further criss-crossed by narrow paths, called 'paths of desire' stretching across the length of the square connecting various points of interest for pedestrians. Granite paving from the previous square, laid out just two years ago, has been recycled in the new design to create paths across the square in every direction while still allowing for the space to host major public events such as festivals, markets, fairs and performances. The new square is an urban magnet with 24-hour activity accurately interpreting Dublin's energy.

Rheinpromenade

Agrippinaufer

Südbrücke

< Rhein

N

Design Agency: metrobox architekten

Designer: Hendrik Bruns, Jens Bartsch, Jan Sauerborn,
Jochen Robert

Photography: metrobox architekten

Location: Cologne, Germany

KAP 686 – Urban Skate Plaza

General Description:

Cologne Cathedral was completed 130 years ago and for 25 of those years skaters have firmly taken possession of Roncalliplatz in front of the southern facade. During this time, a separate culture was formed and for many, the square became an area that they identified with. However, in recent years the scene has been increasingly viewed as a problem. Established interest groups exerted pressure, and some were of the opinion that skating should simply be banned. In order to solve the conflict, the project "KAP 686", an urban skate plaza has been built on the Rhine.

Design Concept:

The basic design concept was created by overlaying the images associated with the square, its use and its location. People flow through the built-up urban landscape, each like a water droplet in a river. The skaters have made this flow of people into a game. Quiet, long drawn-out stretches with large radiuses alternate with jumping at obstacles, like the flowing and spraying of water in a river.

Design Details:

The implementation of this concept in reality is achieved by overlaying the area with a virtual grid which has uniform building areas at the cross-over points. The grid and building areas represent urban elements and are taken from the urban environment.

However, to turn this stark grouping on a grid into a spontaneous arrangement that is optimal for this sport, the area had to be reorganized using a particular algorithm.

This turned the building areas into structures of different sizes; they rise out of the landscape or sink into it to intersperse the space with green elements, meadows and trees. The basic structures are skate objects made from concrete and stand like stones covered by water in a river of flagstones. The ground combines with the skate objects using a template.

The small hard skateboard wheels require a surface that is as level and smooth as possible and does not cause grazing in the event of falls while ensuring the non-slip quality of the public square when it rains.

The incline of the area must ensure Rhine flood water and rain run off completely, while not being too steep for skating. Skaters' jumps as well as hard winters and flooding must not affect the quality of the square over the long term, which is ensured by its construction and the selection of materials.

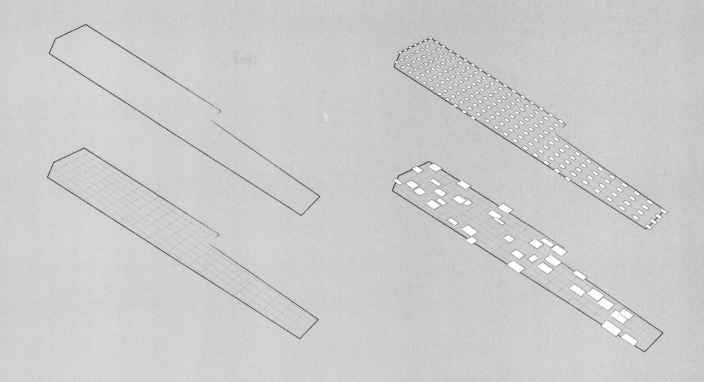

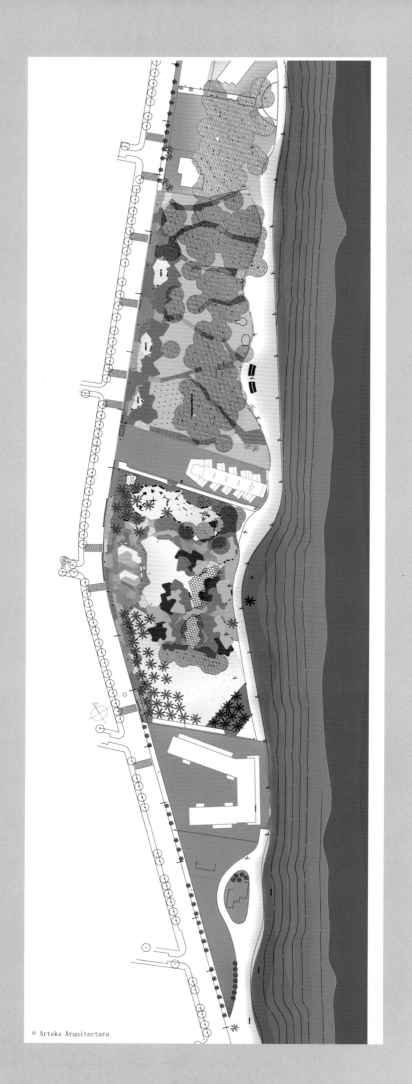

Design Agency: ARTEKS Arquitectura

Designer: Gerard Veciana, Elisabeth Faura

Photography: Pedro Pegenaute

Location: La Pineda, Tarragona, Spain

Area: 28, 000 m²

Park "Pinar de Perruquet"

General Description:

The coastal pine grove of "piñonero" pine has a great landscape and ecological value, and is a habitat to the preserving of the community interest. However, the pine grove has suffered heavy urban development pressure since the second half of the last century. In summer, the pine grove receives a population of more than 30,000, which implies a strong pedestrian traffic towards the beaches across the pine groves, and at the same time a strong impact on the soil. Therefore the solution for the protection of the pine grove was to create an artificial shade of a pergola that resembles the semidarkness color of the pine grove.

© Pedro Pegenaute

Design Concept:

An artificial shade of a pergola was created, since it is not possible to replant a pine grove as the existing one. The architects want to treat the rest of the park with textures that speak of the original pine grove shade that we can no longer have. So they look for references inspired by the organic forms of nature. Instead of setting them in a random order, the architects found repetitive modules for the assembling.

Design Details:

Pergola

The pergola is the architectural element that has a more important arboreal modal. Its strong points are the pillars and the crown.

The Pillars

One of the most important characteristics of the pine grove in littoral is their vertical component, lightly inclined to the direction of the dominant winds. This vertical component contrasts with the horizontal horizon.

The architects have wanted that the pillars are very abstract and they have to take neither the color, nor the form nor the texture of the pines, only the inclination of the east wind that is the causer of the inability to plant pines nowadays.

The Crown

Waviness and movement are two interesting features of the crown. The pergola is constructed by a hexagonal mesh, of wavy directive, with a very flexible material: fiber glass, by means of a process of pultrusion. The fiber glass is a not changeable material for the marine corrosion, and has a deformation better than steel. At the same tension, in windy days, the whole cover of the pergola almost will move.

The pergola has different categories of structure. It has the first structure of reinforcement about the pillars, the second hexagonal structure that gives the waviness, and a third structure of shade based on a few strips of fiber glass with hexagonal mesh that gives an added shade.

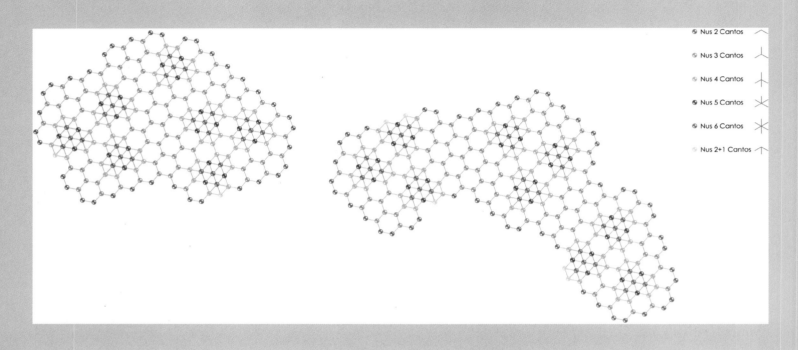

- Nus 2 Cantos
- Nus 3 Cantos
- Nus 4 Cantos
- Nus 5 Cantos
- Nus 6 Cantos
- Nus 2+1 Cantos

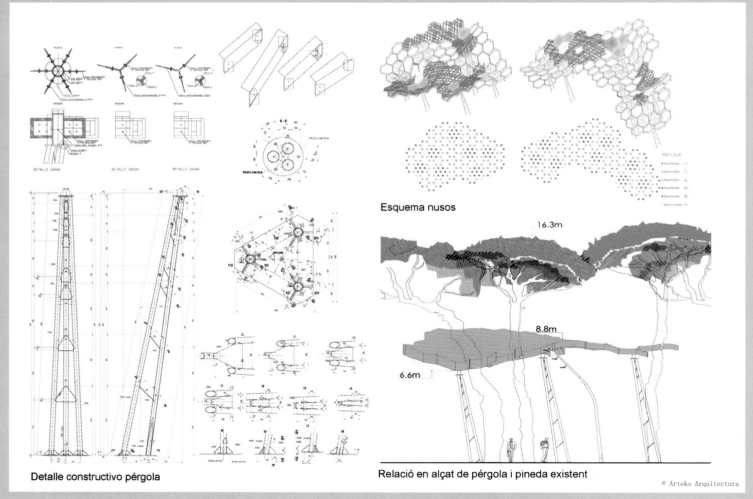

Esquema nusos

16.3m

8.8m

6.6m

Detalle constructivo pérgola

Relació en alçat de pérgola i pineda existent

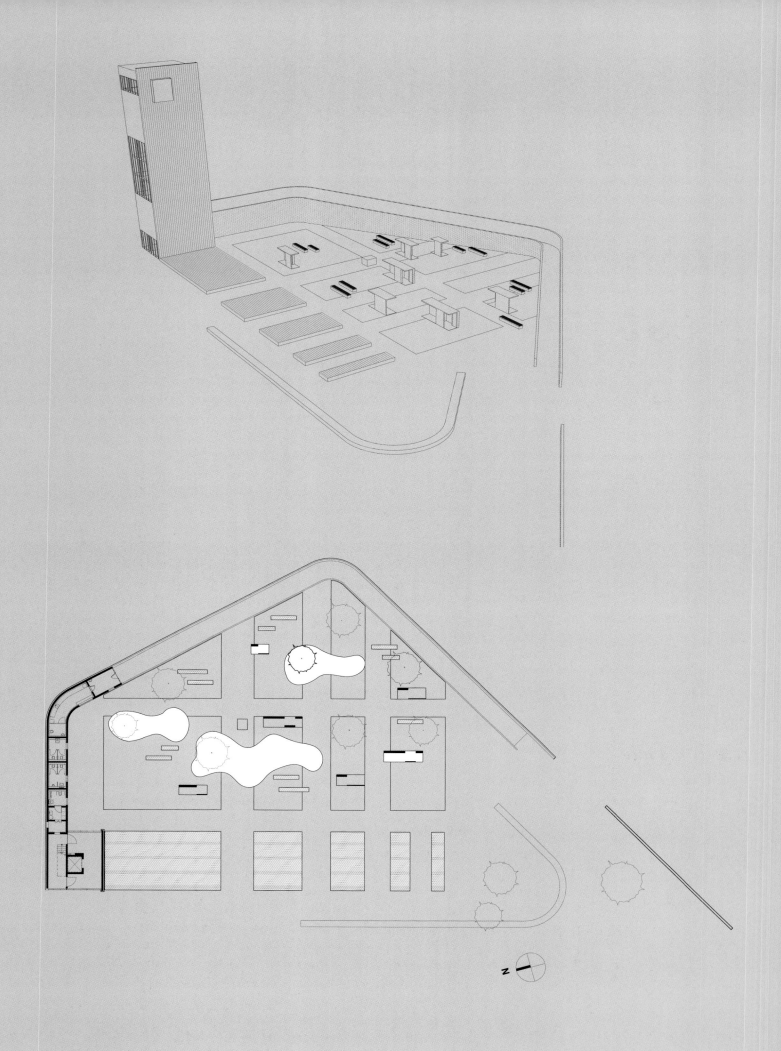

Design Agency: Saunders Architecture

Designer: Todd Saunders

Photography: Bent René Synnevåg

Location: Sarpsborg, Norway

Area: 2,000 m²

Solberg Tower and Rest Area

General Description:

Sarpsborg is a green, flat and calm piece of South Norway and a traditional stopover for travellers on the route to and from Sweden. Underlining the area's natural and historical attractions, supported by strong architectural forms, Saunders carried out the project, a complex, in direct response to both the clients' and site's requirements.

Design Concept:

Focusing on the site and aiming to identify its challenges and advantages in order to define its problems and opportunities, Saunders worked closely with the client, not only to develop the optimum design solution, but also the project's own brief. The architecture came out of what the client needed.

Design Details:

As Sarpsborg is one of the first tastes of Norway the travelers from Sweden experience, it was important for the client that the travelers would be able to slow down and spend time discovering the surrounding nature. The local forest and coastline form a beautiful, yet largely unknown part of the country. The neighboring highway's speed and noise only enhance the traveler's need for a break and re-connection with nature, so a green resting space was on the top of the list. A low walled ramp spirals around the rest area, defining the 2,000 sq m area's limits, while spring-flowering fruit trees adorn the courtyard. Within it, Saunders designed seven small pavilions working with graphic designer Camilla Holcroft, showcasing information on the local rock carvings from the Bronze Age, an exhibition, which continues on the ramp's walls.

Saunders said the surrounding forest is full of rock carvings but no one knows about them because everybody just drives through trying to get to Oslo. The structures also offer the option for temporary artist exhibitions. The flatness of the landscape meant that the beauty of the surrounding nature could only be enjoyed from a

certain height, so the creation of a tower quickly became a main part of the brief. The ramp's asymmetrical walls rise from 0 – 4m, then forms a 30m simple nine–story-tall structure on the site's northern edge, including only a staircase and an elevator. Named Solberg (which translates into "sun mountain"), the tower's aerial views towards the nearby coastline and the Oslo fjord are truly dramatic.

Finally, the design's style and aesthetic was developed in relation to the environs' existing architecture; minimal and geometrical contemporary shapes were chosen, contrasting the local farming villages' more traditional forms. The main materials used were beautifully-ageing CorTen steel for the exterior walls and warm oiled hard wood for the courtyard's design elements and information points. Local slates and fine gravels pave the ground level.

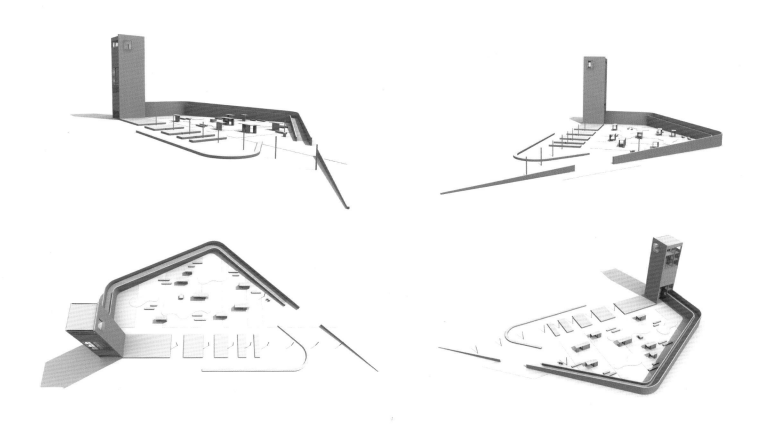

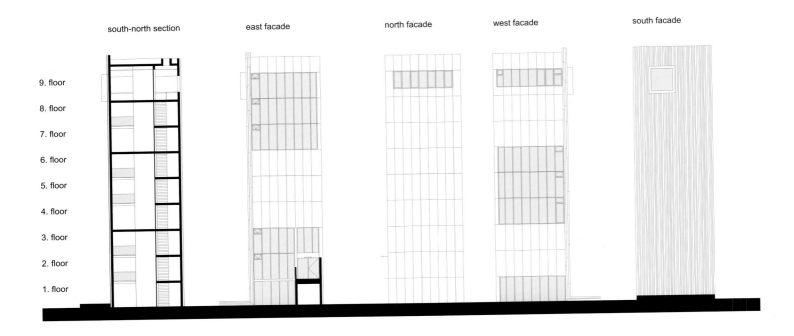

south-north section   east facade   north facade   west facade   south facade

9. floor
8. floor
7. floor
6. floor
5. floor
4. floor
3. floor
2. floor
1. floor

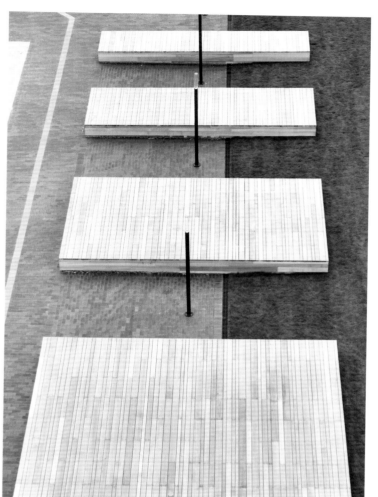

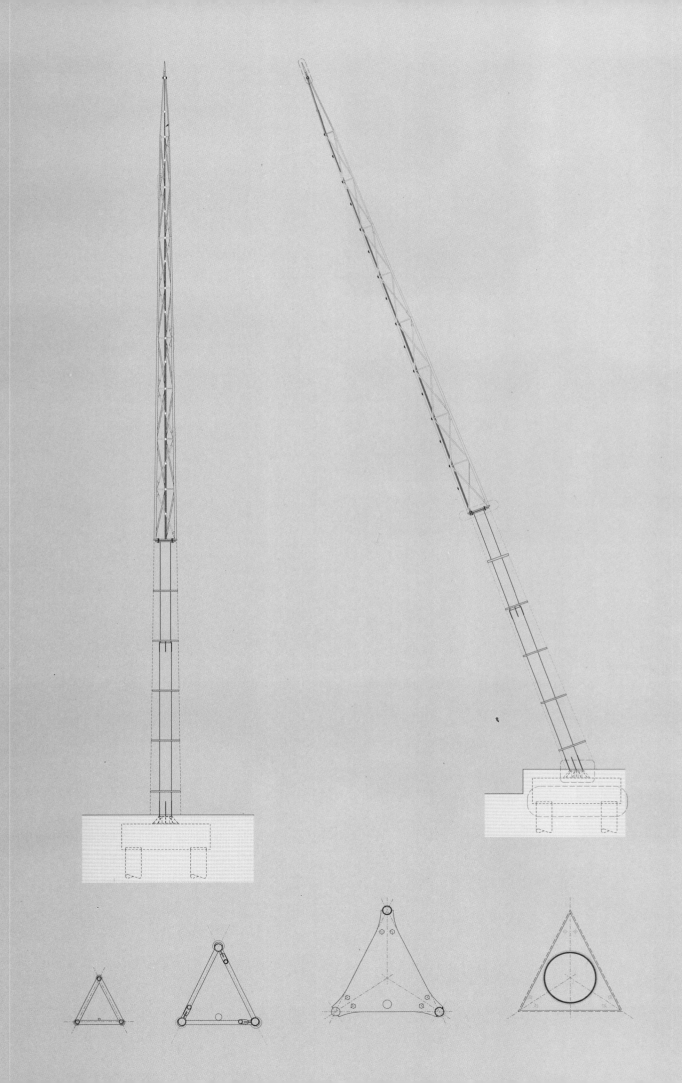

Design Agency: FoRM Associates
Photography: FoRM Associates
Location: Liverpool, UK
Area: 2,000 m²

Mersey Wave

General Description:

The Mersey Wave, a visually dramatic 30 m high and 72 m long gateway, is located on the geographical boundary of Liverpool City in close proximity to the Jaguar Halewood plant.

Design Concept:

The Mersey Wave is uniquely the first urban gateway of its kind designed to be experienced both from moving cars as well as by pedestrian and it marks the geographic boundary of Liverpool.

Design Details:

The geometry of the Mersey Wave gateway is formed by a parallel two-sided progression of six 30 m long fins at graduated angles from the vertical forming a continuous dynamic waveform. The two central fins form a clear and distinct gateway threshold marking the entry in and exit from Liverpool.

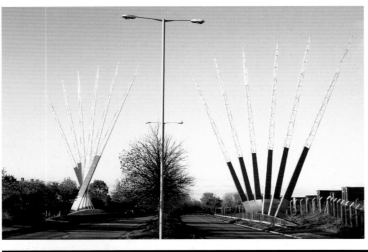

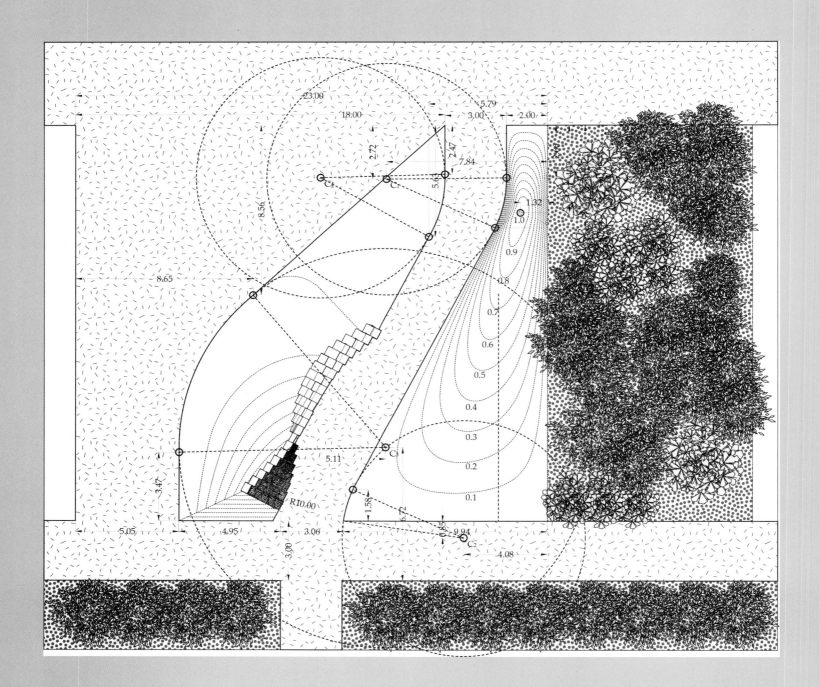

Design Agency: asensio-mah

Designer: Leyre Asensio Villoria, David Syn Chee Mah

Photography: asensio-mah

Location: Quebec, Canada

Area: 200 m²

Surface Deep

General Description:

Surface Deep is a new garden recently installed within the entry sequence for the visitors to the Reford Gardens' Metis International Garden Festival in Quebec, Canada.

Design Concept:

The surface is intended to invite visitors to find many personal ways to engage in, colonize and interact with the garden (from interacting with its micro moss surface to appropriating the whole surface as a ground). Revisiting the garden wall, an element that has been a consistent expressive element within the history of gardening, the entry wall is transformed to form a twisted ribbon-like surface with the help of associative design and modeling techniques. Its undulating form is a response to and gesture for a new entry sequence, framing the entry procession while also embedding an experimental moss garden within its surface.

Design Details:

The surface flips in function and association between a wall, a ground and a cover while creating multiple orientations and different micro-climates for the moss garden. The surface's multiple orientations offer a number of different growing environments for the moss, from slopes exposed to sunlight to constantly

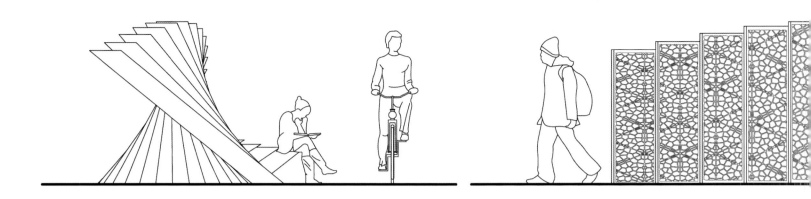

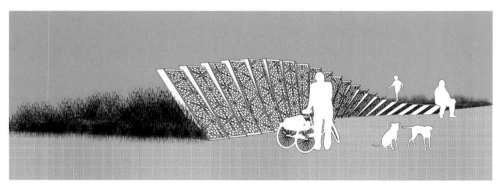

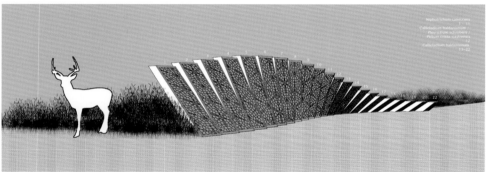

shaded overhangs. These micro-climates informed the distribution of a number of moss species specific to each condition, where the first 11 units were made with Niphotrichum canescens (a sun-loving species), unit 12 is planted with Callicladium haldanianum while the other units remaining (13 to 22) were made with a mixture of Callicladium haldanianum and other shade-loving, forest species such as Pleurozium schreberii, Ptilium crista-castrensis and others. Prior to installation, components of the garden were prefabricated in Cambridge, utilizing the various digital fabrication technologies as well as hand crafting facilities available at the Harvard GSD's fabrication laboratory. Following the fabrication process, the garden was assembled, formed and planted on site at the Reford Gardens over a two week period.

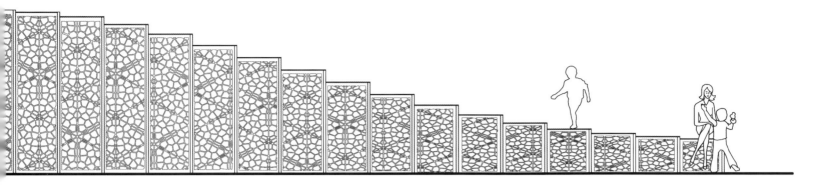

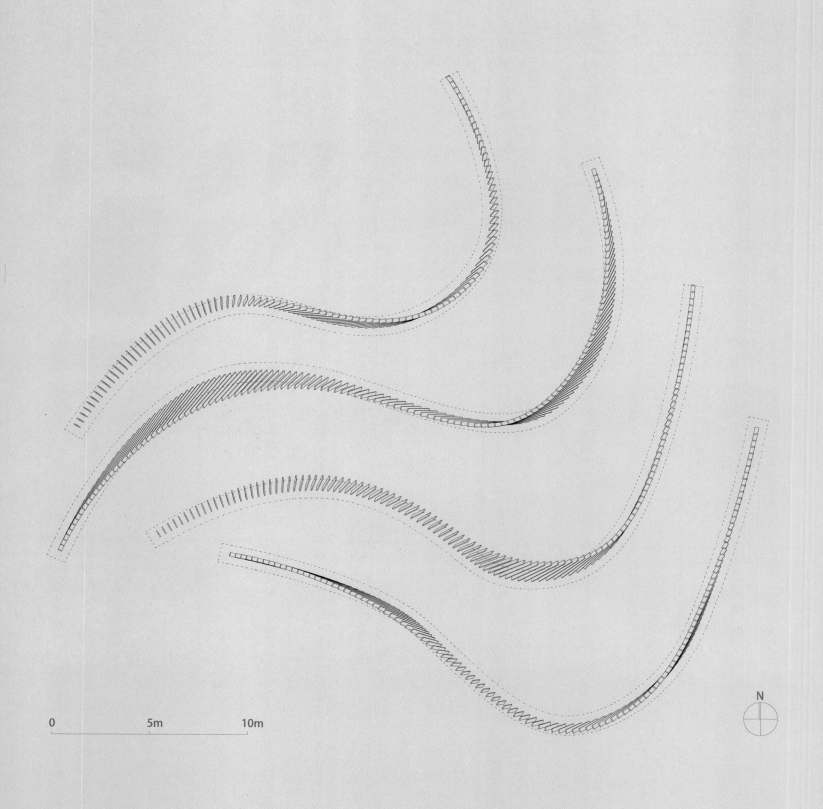

0   5m   10m

N

Design Agency: McChesney Architects
Designer: Ian McChesney
Photography: Peter Cook
Location: Middlesbrough, UK
Area: 2,800 m²

330-335

Blaze

General Description:

Blaze has been designed to populate the disparate roadside verges of the A66 in Middlesbrough — this is the first phase of the piece which can be implemented at numerous locations along the roadside.

Design Concept:

Blaze was conceived as a unifying treatment to the roadside which would gradually emerge along further stretches gradually providing Middlesbrough A66 with its own unique identity.

Design Details:

The form of Blaze was developed using simple array tools within Rhinoceros software providing the basic layout and form. The model was then rationalized and analyzed using Grasshopper software which allowed the production of spreadsheets containing all the data needed to manufacture the staves, including exact coordinate position, lengths and XY angles. This information was made available at tender stage meaning that fabricators knew exactly the number of staves and their precise length.

Blaze was constructed and installed by Chris Brammall who helped to develop the stave mountings. It would be important for the angle of each stave to remain adjustable when installing on site, and so to allow for this, Chris developed a pivoting bracket detail allowing minute adjustments to be made before the staves were clamped in place.

The brackets holding the staves were welded to long curved baseplates which were anchored to concrete strip footings. Once the piece was installed in position and all the angles set, the pivoting brackets were welded up to prevent future movement. Installation of the sculpture on site was completed in about ten days. About 1.5 km of aluminum tubing was used in the piece allowing us to specify a non-standard section extruded specially for the project. The staves have an anodized finish which worked out to be cheaper and more attractive than polyester powder coating. Anodizing increases corrosion resistance and wear resistance, while providing the opportunity to introduce a color to the finish of the aluminum.

Once installed, the bases of the staves were buried under a layer of pebbles contained within timber edgings with topsoil reinstated alongside. The ground will be rotavated and seeded in spring.

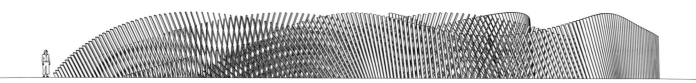

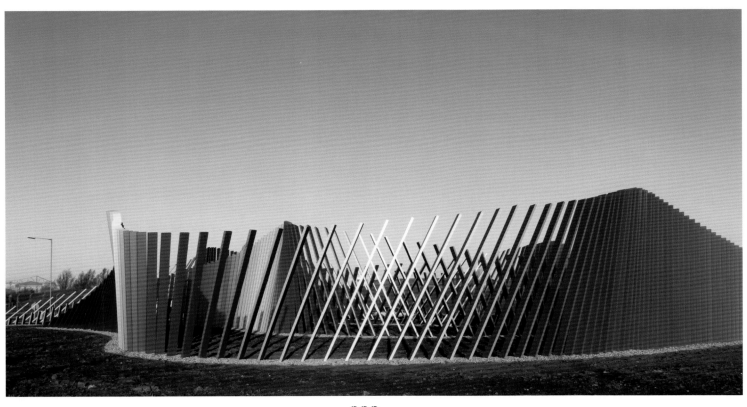

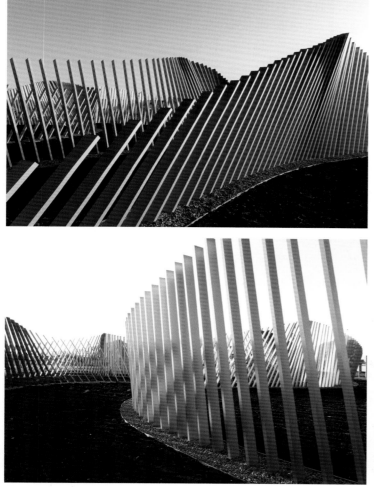

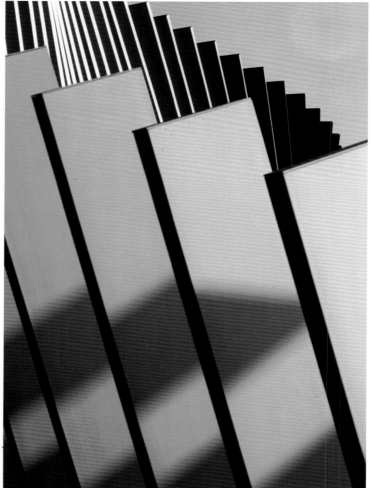

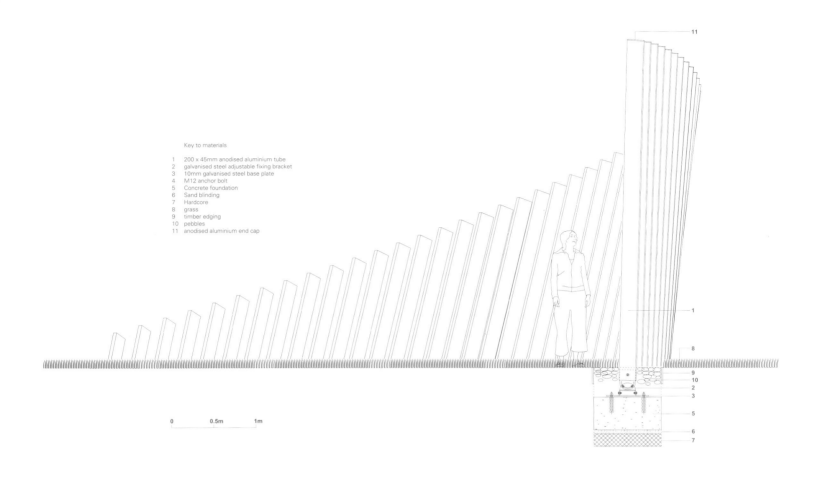

Key to materials

1 200 x 45mm anodised aluminium tube
2 galvanised steel adjustable fixing bracket
3 10mm galvanised steel base plate
4 M12 anchor bolt
5 Concrete foundation
6 Sand blinding
7 Hardcore
8 grass
9 timber edging
10 pebbles
11 anodised aluminium end cap

0   0.5m   1m

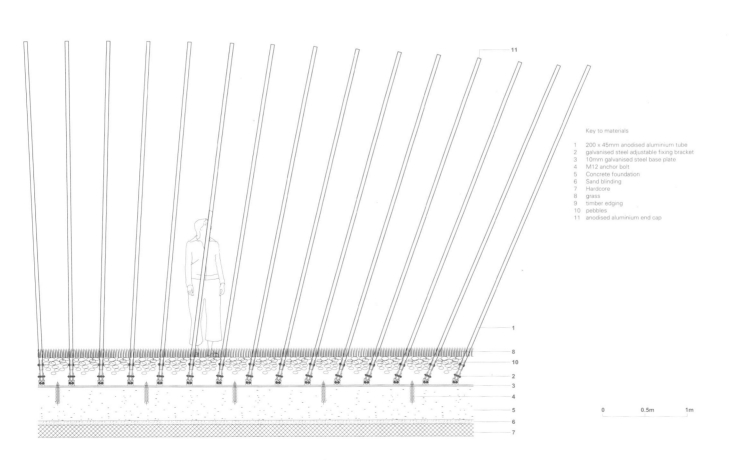

Key to materials

1 200 x 45mm anodised aluminium tube
2 galvanised steel adjustable fixing bracket
3 10mm galvanised steel base plate
4 M12 anchor bolt
5 Concrete foundation
6 Sand blinding
7 Hardcore
8 grass
9 timber edging
10 pebbles
11 anodised aluminium end cap

0   0.5m   1m

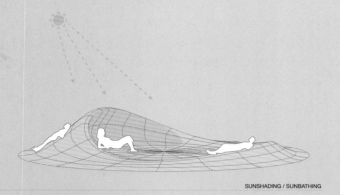

SUNSHADING / SUNBATHING

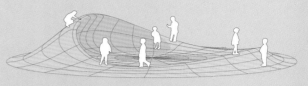

PLAY SPACE

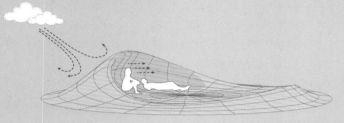

SEA BREEZE PROTECTION / DIFFUSER

COMMUNAL SPACE

APPLICATION DIAGRAM

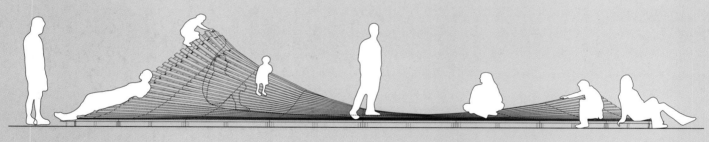

SIDE ELEVATION

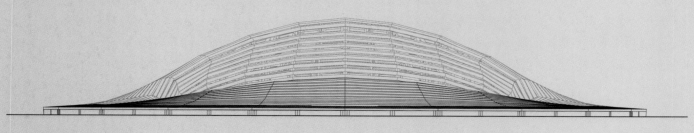

FRONT ELEVATION

Design Agency: 24° Studio

Designer: Fumio Hirakawa, Marina Topunova

Photography: 24° Studio

Location: Kobe, Japan

Area: 78.5 m²

Crater Lake

General Description:

Crater Lake is situated in the manmade Port Island, Shiosai Park that provides a vast view of the Kobe urban center, its surrounding mountains and ocean views. This multi-use environmental installation serves as a meeting place where every area can be used as seating for visitors to contemplate the surroundings, thus invoking a social interaction within and around.

Design Concept:

The design motive was inspired by the history of the Great Hanshin- Awaji Earthquake of 1995 that led to inevitable changes within built environment sparring only the nature that surrounds Kobe. The design intent of Crater Lake installation is to take advantage of this unique location by creating an undulating wooden landscape that provides a variation of open and unconstrained settings with 360° views.

Design Details:

Multiple ideas and materials have been tried to realize the complexity of smooth and undulating form. Wood was chosen for its strong structural capacity, natural qualities and easy to work with.

Every surface may be utilized as seating place. Additional stools are placed in the middle of the space that can be reorganized according to the user's preferences.

The gentle hill surfaces invite people of different generations by providing spatial conditions that allow them to interact with the landscape space like a playground device, relax in the shade of the mount, and socialize.

Standard wood and off-the-shelf hardware were used in construction to avoid any costly customized fabrication process. 2x4 studs were used for all structural members and 30x60 mm treated cedar wood was used for the surface. The circular surface was divided into a number of radial parts, with optimal number of 20 parts. The structure of radial parts consists of series of free-form ribs composed in segmentations with horizontal support and cross bracing for rigidity. Each radial segment has 64 surface planks that are attached to three structural ribs that are rigidly connected between each other with horizontal supports. The surfaces with the most anticipated traffic flow have narrow spacing between each plank.

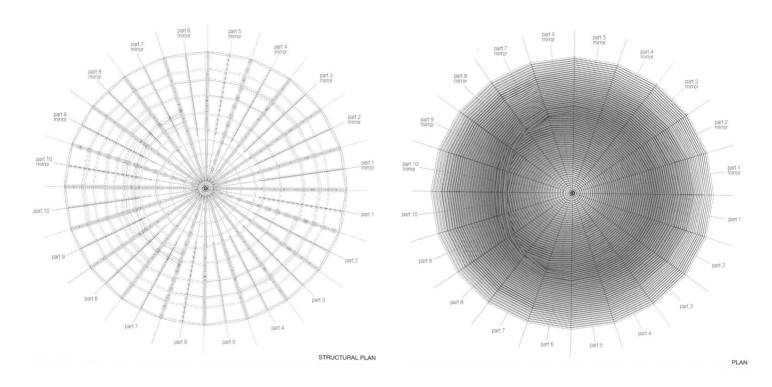

STRUCTURAL PLAN

PLAN

	PART 1 / PART 1 MIRROR	PART 2 / PART 2 MIRROR	PART 3 / PART 3 MIRROR	PART 4 / PART 4 MIRROR	PART 5 / PART 5 MIRROR	PART 6 / PART 6 MIRROR	PART 7 / PART 7 MIRROR	PART 8 / PART 8 MIRROR	PART 9 / PART 9 MIRROR	PART 10 / PART 10 MIRROR
PLANK TYPES										
PLANK LAYOUT										
STRUCTURE										
AXONOMETRIC A										
AXONOMETRIC B										

MATRIX DIAGRAM

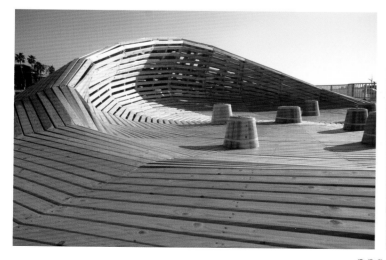

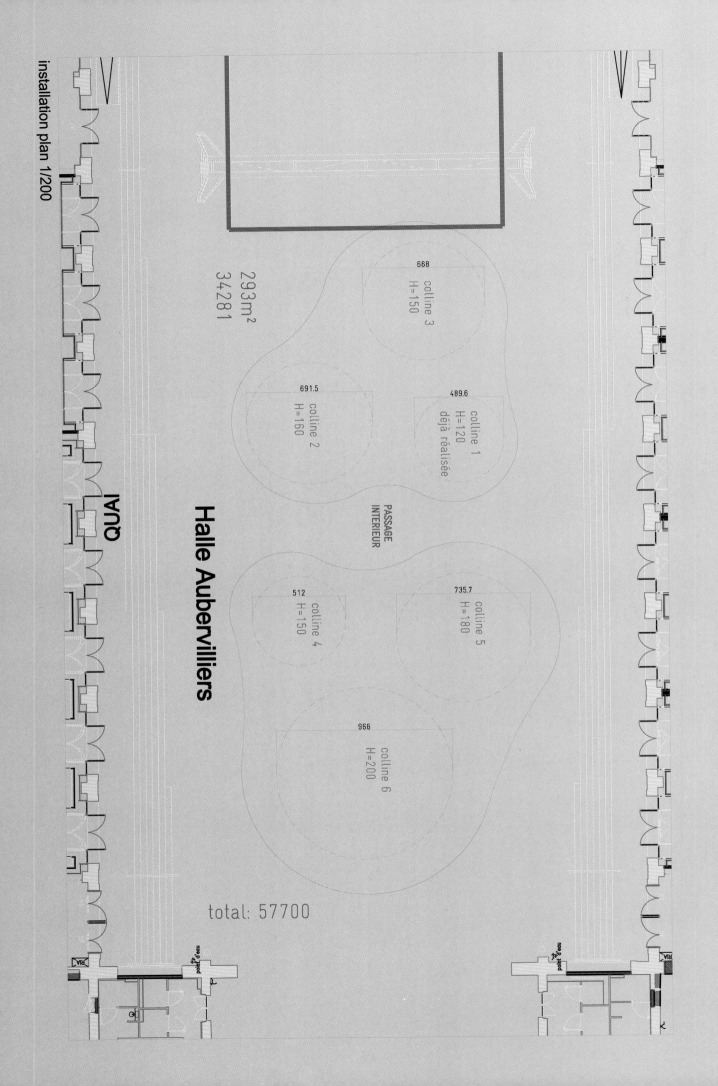

installation plan 1/200

QUAI

Halle Aubervilliers

293m²
34281

668
colline 3
H=150

691.5
colline 2
H=160

489.6
colline 1
H=120
déjà réalisée

PASSAGE
INTERIEUR

512
colline 4
H=150

735.7
colline 5
H=180

966
colline 6
H=200

total: 57700

Designer: Clémence Eliard, Elise Morin
Photography: Elise Morin, Yannick Fradin, Martin Eliard
Location: Paris, France
Area: 500 m²

Waste Landscape

General Description:

Waste Landscape is a 500 square meters artificial undulating landscape covered by an armor of 65,000 unsold or collected CDs, which have been sorted and hand-sewn.

Design Concept:

Waste Landscape will be displayed in locations coherent with the stakes of the project: art role in society, raising consciousness to environmental problems through culture, alternative mode of production and valuation of district associative work and professional rehabilitation.

Design Details:

It is well known that CDs are condemned to gradually disappear from our daily life, and to later participate in the construction of immense open-air, floating or buried toxic waste reception centers. Made of petroleum, this reflecting slick of CDs forms a still sea of metallic dunes: the art work's monumental scale reveals the precious aspect of a small daily object. The project joins a global, innovative and committed approach, from its means of production until the end of its "life".

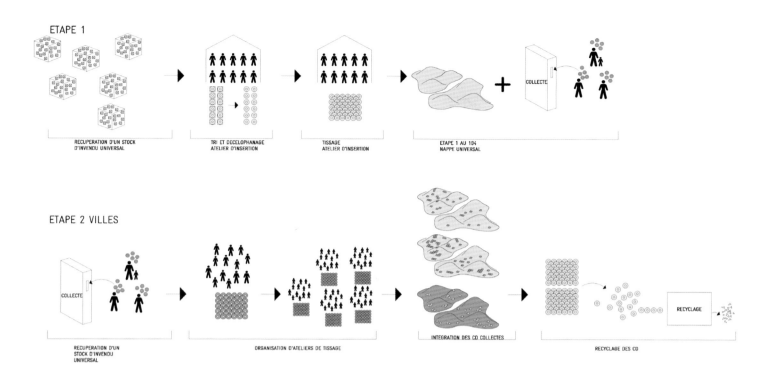

ETAPE 1

RECUPERATION D'UN STOCK
D'INVENDU UNIVERSAL

TRI ET DECELOPHANAGE
ATELIER D'INSERTION

TISSAGE
ATELIER D'INSERTION

ETAPE 1 AU 104
NAPPE UNIVERSAL

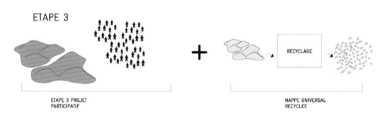

ETAPE 2 VILLES

RECUPERATION D'UN
STOCK D'INVENDU
UNIVERSAL

ORGANISATION D'ATELIERS DE TISSAGE

INTEGRATION DES CD COLLECTES

RECYCLAGE DES CD

ETAPE 3

ETAPE 3 PROJET
PARTICIPATIF

NAPPE UNIVERSAL
RECYCLEE

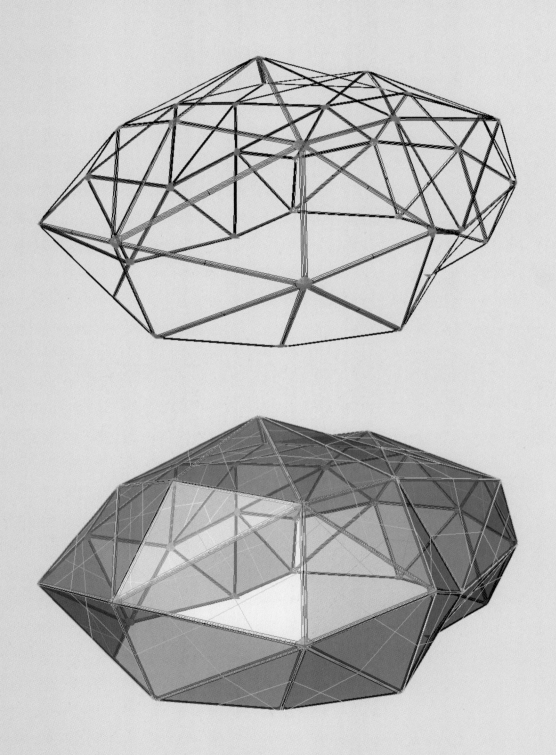

Design Agency: *MARCO HEMMERLING Studio for Spatial Design*

Designer: *Marco Hemmerling*

Photography: *Christian Doppelgatz*

Location: *Cologne, Germany*

Cityscope

General Description:

Cityscope is a crystal-like installation positioned in front of the main station in Cologne, a highly frequented urban square that allows different angles of vision and supports at the same time the interaction of the beholder with the installation.

Design Concept:

Cityscope tries to open the perspective by concentrating different and unusual views of the urban surroundings.

Design Details:

Cityscope deals with the fragmented perception of urban spaces. The beveling structure can be seen as an urban kaleidoscope that reflects fragmented views on the city and composes at the same time a three-dimensional image of the surrounding facades. While moving around the sculpture and the images that reflect on the triangulated envelope, continuously change. In that way the beholder becomes an integral part of the installation and its complex reflections.

The radiant foil, which is applied to the outer skin of the sculpture is dependent on the daylight situation and the position of the beholder, and the lighting colors. The color-transformation generates an intentional alienation that reinforces the idea of a fragmented perception. Like the facades of a city, the specular envelope becomes transparent at night, when the installation is illuminated from the inside. The appearance changes in another transformation process into complementary colors and the inside of the installation will be demonstrated.

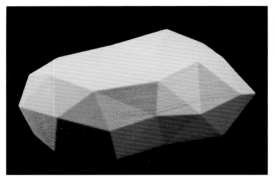
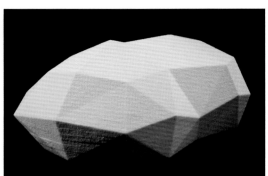

The beveling structure can be seen as an urban kaleidoscope that reflects fragmented views on the city and composes at the same time a three-dimensional image of the surrounding facades.

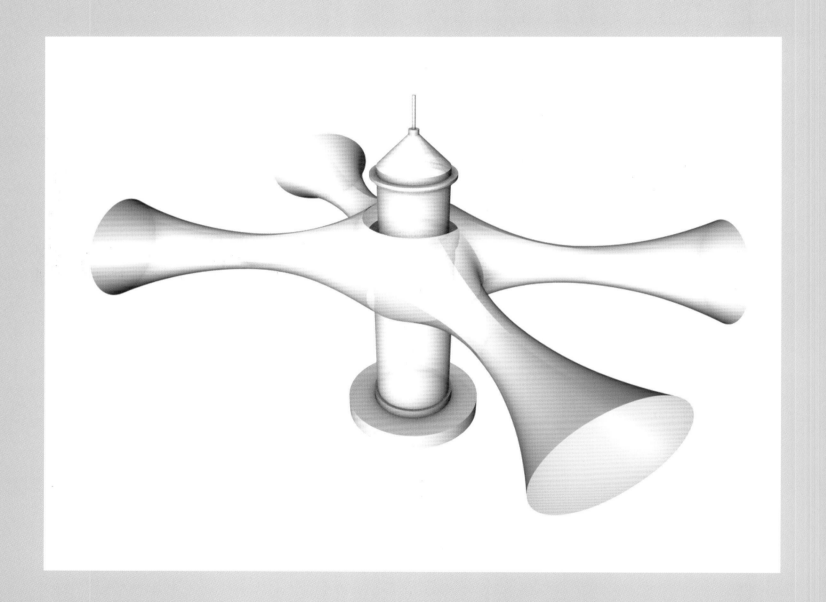

Design Agency: *MARCO HEMMERLING Studio for Spatial Design*

Designer: *Marco Hemmerling*

Photography: *Michel Bobilier*

Location: *Geneva, Switzerland*

Lighttube

General Description:

Lighttube was located at Square Pierre Fatio in the city center and designed for the 9th annual festival "Arbres et Lumières" in Geneva, Switzerland 2009.

Design Concept:

The concept for the illumination is based on two major aspects of spatial perception. First, the installation amplifies the relation between the central column and the surrounding trees. The second aspect of the design aims at an added value, which is brought in with the new element of the Lighttube. It still incorporates a constant change of color for the illuminated trees and the membrane structure to support the idea of evolutionary transformation and generates at the same time an ever-changing perception of the scenery.

Design Details:

By reinforcing the correlation of the trees with the center of the square, the light membrane structure focuses on the connection of the vertical elements of the site. Even though being a connector, the Lighttube manages to establish its own quality, which formally derives from the evolutionary principle of growth. The abstract idea of ramification is transformed into an integral shape that puts the trees as well as the column and the space in between in a new light.

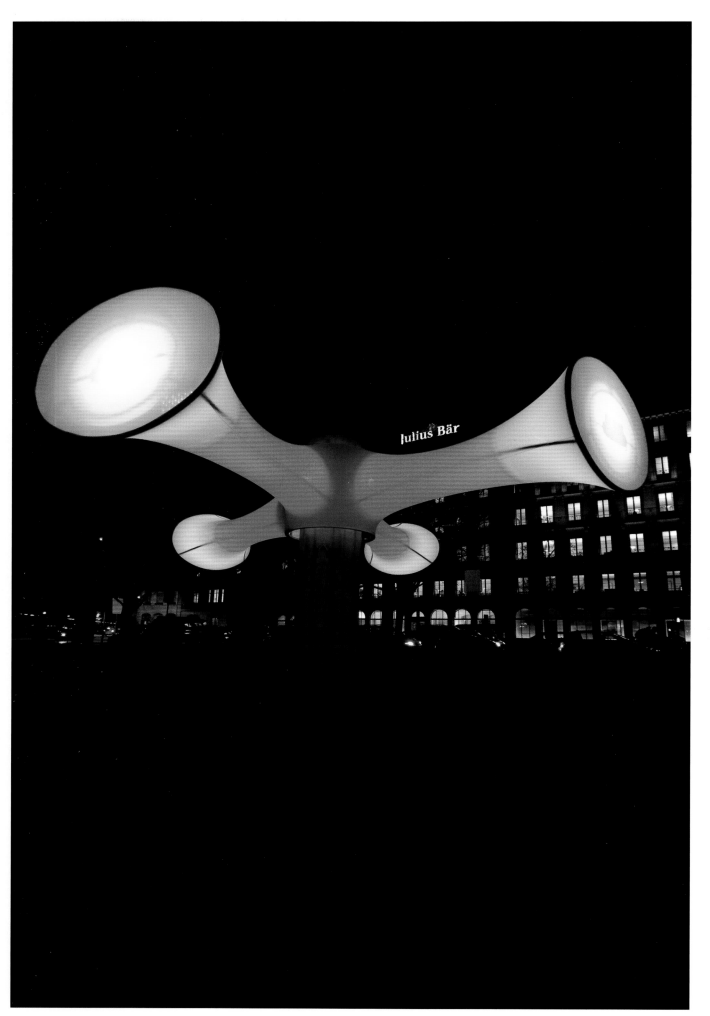

SENDPOINTS PUBLISHING

www.sendpoint.com.cn

SHOW TIME
–TOP DISPLAY AND STAGE DESIGN

ISBN: 978-988-15624-8-7

Binding: Hardcover

Size: 220×300mm

Pages: 312p

Language: English

GREAT TRANSFORMATION
–Head Office Space

ISBN: 978-988-18923-6-2

Binding: Hardcover

Size: 250×250mm

Pages: 356p

Language: English

WELCOME
–GLOBAL EXCELLENT STORE DISPLAY DESIGN

ISBN: 978-988-19610-8-2

Binding: Hardcover

Size: 210×280mm

Pages: 324p

Language: English

CLOSE TO ARCHITECTURE

ISBN: 978-988-18923-5-5

Binding: Hardcover

Size: 245×315mm

Pages: 424p

Language: English

OFFICE DESIGN

ISBN: 978-988-15624-1-8

Binding: Hardcover

Size: 235×310mm

Pages: 376p

Language: English

LANDSCAPE ART – VILLA

ISBN: 978-988-19842-1-0

Binding: Hardcover

Size: 245×385mm

Pages: 334p

Language: English

SHOPPING PARDISE

ISBN: 978-988-19610-6-8

Binding: Hardcover

Size: 280×280mm

Pages: 308p

Language: English

GREEN OFFICE BULIDING

ISBN: 978-988-19842-2-7

Binding: Hardcover

Size: 260×240mm

Pages: 314p

Language: English

SendPoints

SendPoints Guangzhou
T/+86-20-89095121

SendPoints Beijing
T/+86-10-84139071

SendPoints Shanghai
T/+86-21-63523469

Online store:
sendpointsbooks.taobao.com